JUST ONE GUY'S STORIES

Fred Mayfield

WORDS MATTER
P U B L I S H I N G
OUR WORDS CHANGE THE WORLD

Words Matter Publishing
P.O. Box 1190
Decatur, IL 62525
www.wordsmatterpublishing.com

ISBN: 978-1-958000-48-9

Library of Congress Number: 2023937788

DEDICATION

I want to dedicate Just One Guy's Stories to my late mother, Mary Sue Mayfield "Mamaw," the most kind, loving, caring, and positive person I've ever known. She always believed in me and said that I could accomplish anything I wanted to in life. Everyone that was blessed to know her will confirm that she was a living angel that God put on this earth as evidence that those who believe in him and follow His word would make anyone they touch feel His presence. Even though it was a sad day when she went to Heaven, God was so happy He cried when she arrived. This world has had many wonderful mothers throughout time, and like my mother, they are all in Heaven wearing their wings and looking down on us, just waiting until we are with them again.

ACKNOWLEDGMENTS

I want to acknowledge our good friend Tammy Koelling of Words Matter Publishing, who inspired me to write Just One Guy's Stories. Her confidence and enthusiasm gave me the push I needed to become an Author. I have always loved writing and telling stories, but I never dreamed I would be able to share them with the world until I met Tammy.

I would also like to acknowledge my best friend since I was in diapers, Bob Mezzetti. Without him, I would have never had most of my wonderful experiences or gotten in as much trouble. Even though I didn't have an actual brother, Bob has always been closer to me than anyone else. He has always been and always will be my brother.

Belief in yourself is very important, but having wonderful people who believe in you, helps you focus on your tasks and not give up during your journey. This has been one of the best journeys I've ever been on!

CONTENTS

CHASING THE FOG

There are a lot of things we didn't worry or know about growing up. We used to ride our bikes all day and night over the neighborhood. When we weren't riding our bikes, we would walk everywhere. Whether we walked to the store, the park, or the cinema, we never worried about our safety. Looking back, I realize how blessed we were not to have to worry about the kinds of dangers kids have today.

Our biggest worry was wrecking our bike, falling down and scrapping our knee, or maybe getting in trouble if we didn't get home by the time our parents told us to. I don't remember my parents ever being worried about where we went or what we were doing. Being children before cellphones and tracking devices, our parents had to trust us to be smart and stay out of trouble.

The most dangerous thing we ever did was to get on an old paint pony that a man would bring door to door to take pictures on. I remember riding our bikes in some pretty dangerous ways, but it didn't feel dangerous to us. It was fun. We even ran behind a smog truck spraying fog to kill mosquitos. We would chase that fog truck all the way down the street. I don't know what was in a fog, but I don't remember any of us ever getting sick, though it did smell a little funny.

The kids of today have no idea about the fun we were able to have back then. I miss those days.

CHRISTMAS GROWING UP

~

Growing up, Christmas was one of my favorite times of the year. We would travel to my grandparent's house on Christmas Eve, as did my aunts, uncles, and cousins on my dad's side of the family. We would play with fireworks, look at Christmas lights, and open gifts from each other that night. When we were done, we would go to my other grandparent's house to spend Christmas with all my aunts, uncles, and cousins on my mom's side of the family.

It seems like every Christmas back then, I was sick Christmas morning for some reason. I remember getting up and seeing all the cool gifts and going right back to bed. What kid would turn away from Christmas gifts to return to bed? My mom's family was much bigger than my dad's family, so we got a lot of presents. We had a lot of food and amazing pies from the famous bakery in town as well as all kinds of fruit.

As we got older and our grandparents passed away, we would spend Christmas at home. We would get so excited over what gifts we would receive it was hard to sleep. I'm not going to say we were spoiled, but we always seemed to get what we wanted for Christmas. It was such an amazing feeling waking up Christmas morning and seeing all the gifts stacked up everywhere. The older we got, the gifts were better quality and less quantity but that was okay because I think those gifts came from the store and didn't cost Santa anything.

We opened all our gifts before digging into our stockings. They were always full of gifts, candy, fruit, and nuts. While we played with all our new presents, my mom would make the second-best meal of the year. Thanksgiving was the first.

Looking back on the memories and traditions, I am so thankful to have been able to share them with my family. To this day, a sound or a smell takes me back to Christmas growing up.

FINBARR AND BULLET

~

Growing up in the city, I saw a lot of things, but some things were truly unforgettable. One of the things I often did was go to the dam at the creek after it rained to watch the alligator gars floating around.

There was this one time after a storm when the water was really muddy and flowing fast. It was flowing so fast it was a little scary, but something seemed to draw me close to it to feel the power of the water. One time I was looking up, and there were a whole lot of water moccasins floating on top of the water. There were so many; I started backing up really slowly when I felt something on the back of my neck. I turned around slowly to find myself face-to-face with a whole nest of water moccasins in a bush. I moved back slowly and ran all the way home, scared to death.

My best friend and I lived pretty close, which was great. I would go see him often, and we would ride our bikes everywhere. There was an undeveloped place nearby that we made bike paths through all the time.

He had a dog named Stranger that was pretty smart. Every once in a while, Stranger would bring home baby rabbits in his mouth. He didn't ever hurt them; he would just find them somewhere in that undeveloped land and bring them home with him. We would always take them back to the area we think he found them and hoped they would be okay. When we went back, they were always gone, but we never really knew what had happened to them.

One boy in the neighborhood had gotten shot in the mouth by someone down at the creek. He could push his tongue from the inside to his upper lip, and there would pop out a perfect cylindrical shape of a pellet. Another boy, who was rather strange, would pull all his eyelashes out.

I guess one of the weirdest and funniest things I ever saw was at another one of my friend's houses. We would go to parties there, and they had a small pesky little monkey named Finbarr that used to basically run wild in the house. He would dip his hand in the punch bowl and get a drink before running off. He was also bad about eating off your plate when you weren't paying attention.

The funniest thing I ever saw Finbarr do was to ride on the back of their dog, Bullet. Bullet's head was turned sideways all the time because I think something happened to one of his ears. You would see Finbarr riding on the back of Bullet all the time, but it didn't look like Bullet was enjoying it as much as Finbarr. I loved seeing that.

One day I went over to visit, and Finbarr wasn't around. When we asked what happened to him, they said that Bullet finally got tired of him riding on his back, and now there's no more Finbarr. I didn't ask anymore as I didn't want to hear something bad happen to him. I always smile when I think back to that time.

FIREWORKS

Growing up, I used to love popping fireworks. I remember my mom taking my best friend and me to a lake nearby every 4th of July to pop fireworks. We lived in town, so we weren't supposed to pop them there, but the lake was out of the city limits, so it was okay. We had every firework a young boy loved, from bottle rockets and flare guns to cherry bombs and smoke bombs. We'd end our evenings with sparklers. We would run around the lake waving them and laughing. There was this one firework that was snake-like. It was like this black thing that grew longer as it burned. It was so much fun! Somehow my mom seemed to know exactly how many fireworks were needed to wear us out.

It wasn't just shooting fireworks with my friend; we also watched the town's fireworks show downtown. Our fireworks were nothing compared to the towns. Their fireworks lit up the night sky. My favorite was the grand finale. They shot off so many fireworks. There was a loud bang as the night sky became a rainbow of colors. I always left feeling excitement and joy.

It wasn't just on the fourth we had fireworks. I remember going to my grandmothers during Christmas with my cousins and me. We would take cans, nut shells, and pretty much anything else we could find to blow up that wouldn't get us in trouble. There were a few times when the fireworks would blow up in my hand. It hurt my ears and scared me, but no real damage was done. My cousins were older than me, and they would chase me with bottle rockets, flairs, and firecrackers until my grandmother would finally tell them to stop.

My best friend's brother was really smart and used to somehow make gunpowder himself. He would pour it into a glass vial, and it would erupt like a flair. It was so cool that my best friend and I thought we would do the same thing. Of course, we didn't know how to make gunpowder, so we took a whole bunch of firecrackers and emptied the gunpowder onto a piece of paper. Then we found a glass breath saver bottle and poured all the gunpowder in it. We stuck a fuse in it and were going to light the fuse and watch it flair up as his brother's did, but there was one thing we didn't know. The glass breath-saver bottle had a small one-way entry so that the breath-saver drops would only drip out. When we put the fuse in the bottle, there was no room for the gunpowder to flair out.

I was sitting on a chair on our back porch, about to light it, but right when I was going to do it, my best friend started to run away. He's the one who had the idea and said it would work, so I stopped and asked why he was running away. He said he was just kidding and it would be okay. I told him that I wasn't going to light it if he was going to run away. Of course, he said he wouldn't, but as soon as I lit it, he ran away, and before I could get out of the chair, "BOOM!" It was the loudest thing I've ever heard! The bottle just disintegrated. I never could hear the same out of my right ear again. I was so mad at my best friend for running off and leaving me to lite the "BOMB"!

My big sister ran outside and thought I had shot my best friend, but I didn't even have a gun. If I had one, I might have, though! I guess God was watching over us because nothing got damaged except my right ear, of course.

I learned a lot of lessons throughout my life about fireworks. I now realize that though they are fun, they can be very dangerous if you don't be careful what you're doing.

HIGH SCHOOL MEMORIES

I have a lot of memories of high school. I think about some of the life experiences I had back then with fond memories. When I was a freshman, I learned about being initiated into the football team through firsthand experience. The older classmen would put hot gel cream in our jocks. We didn't know until we were out of the locker room and on the field. It would burn so badly all the way through practice. We were picked on and made fun of all the time by the upperclassmen.

When I was a sophomore, I learned about getting to class on time. One of my best friends and I used to call in an order to a burger place close to the school. We would run there and quickly eat it before heading back to school. Most of the time, we made it back just in time for the bell to be in class. There were some occasions we were a little late, nothing more than a few seconds at most. But it didn't matter how late we were; the teacher would write us up. When we accumulated too many, we were sent to the office.

Since I played football, I couldn't make detention after school, so the office told my coach, and he found a way to punish me. I'll never forget my dad showing up at the school because I was late getting home, only to find me running around and around the track in full pads with my coach watching. My dad and the coach just watched me keep running until he felt I had learned my lesson and let me go to the locker room. I thought my dad was going to kill me, but I think he knew I had learned my lesson, so he didn't say anything. I know one thing; I was never late to class again.

By the time I was a junior, a new high school had been built. This is the place I had my first real girlfriend. She was a year younger than me. She was in the band; I was on the football team; it was a good match.

When I was a senior, I started thinking about life and my future, as most graduating seniors do. There were a lot of disappointments that year. It started off great; we won most of our football games, but unfortunately, we started losing. Sadly, we didn't end up winning the city championship.

At the end of the year, we had our sports banquet. The main award was Player of the Year. This was the award the team chose. I was well-liked, and I just knew they would chose me. Even our trainer said he saw the ballots, and 90% of them were for me. I was so excited. I worked hard every year to be a leader for the team. When our head coach announced the winner, it wasn't me; it was one of our running backs. Everyone was shocked and didn't say anything. I stood up and clapped for him, and everyone else joined in.

When the coach announced that I was a close runner-up, the whole crowd blew up and cheered. Later I found out that the coach picked him instead of me because he thought he would have a better chance of getting a scholarship as his parents couldn't afford to pay for his college. I learned a hard lesson that day.

High school had a lot of memories. Some were good and some bad, but I will always remember them.

It's So Hard to Say Goodbye

Growing up, I didn't have any dogs as pets. I don't think my dad cared for them that much. I did have chickens and ducks, but they were only around at Easter. I used to play with my best friend's dogs sometimes. I remember this one time his dog had puppies. They were so small and cute. I wanted one really bad. I started to take one home until my best friend's big brother asked me what I was doing. I told him she said I could have one, but he made me put it back. I don't know what I was thinking because I knew my dad wouldn't have let me keep it anyway.

When I was a little older, after we moved, I had a cat that I named "Smokey" because he was a kind of dark gray. I loved him. One day he left and never came back. I never knew what had happened to him, but it made me very sad.

After I grew up and got married, my wife wanted a dog. She is an animal lover. She grew up with them. I couldn't say no, so we got our first dog, a Shih Tzu. As life went on and we moved from place to place, we finally settled on some land in the country. There were always stray dogs that people used to just drop off and leave behind that ended up at our house. My wife always felt sorry for them, and they ended up staying with us. Through the years, we have had many different kinds and sizes of dogs as well as other animals too. Most of them were usually ones that people gave us because they didn't want them or couldn't take care of them.

Eventually, we had two goats, a miniature donkey, and a horse that belonged to my daughter. We also ended up with three parrots too. Two from one home and one my mother-in-law no longer wanted. If you have ever had an animal, you know that they are in many ways like children and depend on you to take care of them. In return, they are always happy to see you, whether you're gone for a short time or a long time. They are also always there for you when you're sad. I guess they can just tell when you're hurting, and they always make you feel better because you know they can always tell and care.

Through the years, I think I got closer to my animals than I was to most of the people I knew. Animals have an unconditional love for their owners, no matter how you're feeling, so your heart just gets attached to them. Over time they all get older, like everything else in life, and you end up having to let them go. I know animals all go to heaven because they are such a blessing during their lives. It was always so hard to say goodbye because you never wanted them to go, and they never wanted to leave you. I believe they know, though, that they will see you again in heaven one day and will love you there forever.

LIGHTS AND COLORS IN THE SKY

~

When I was really young, I remember looking up at the night sky in wonderment. There were so many lights in the sky, but I didn't know what they were. Someone once told me that the big light in the sky at night was the Moon, and the big light in the sky during the day was the Sun. At the time, I was too young to go to school, so I didn't know what all the lights were. One night, I asked my mom what the lights in the sky were. She told me they were called stars. She tried to explain the different constellations, but I didn't understand them until I got older.

I can still remember when I saw my first rainbow. It had just rained, and the sun was starting to come out a little bit. I was so excited I ran into the house and told my mom that there were colors in the sky. She came out and told me it was called a rainbow and was God's promise never to flood the world again. I was too young to understand what she was saying until I got older and started reading the Bible. The world is such a wonderful place with lights in the sky at night and colors during the day. It's so cool how you don't know what anything is when you're born and how amazed you are when you learn what everything is as you grow up. If only we could keep that wonder as we grow older.

MY BEST FRIEND BOB

~

I grew up in a small city in a small house on a small street. My mom's best friend, Jodi, lived two houses down on the same side of the street. She had a son named Bob. We started playing together when we were in diapers. We had many life experiences together growing up. I remember my mom telling me that Jodi was watching me one day, and she laid me down on the warm dryer to change my cloth diaper, because there were no plastic diapers back then. When she opened my diaper, I shot a stream that landed all the way to the table and right in her coffee. I'm sure my mom and Jodi had a lot of stories like that through the years.

I remember getting ducks for Easter one year. Once they grew up, we couldn't keep them anymore, so we gave them to our housekeeper. She lived in the country with a pond they could play in. She used to bring us duck eggs sometimes. I thought that was neat, as it was my ducks they came from.

Another year, I got baby chickens. Around Easter, they would color the babies, but I don't think the dye hurt them. They grew out of those colors and ended up looking like regular chickens. I don't remember what happened to them. I guess my mom may have given them to our housekeeper too.

Bob and I used to play outside all the time. Back then, we didn't have any video games or computers. I don't remember much being on TV except Soap Operas. We used our imaginations and played like we were in the army or going on some kind of adventure. Sometimes my dad would bring a big box home from somewhere, and we would use it to play like we were in a submarine underwater.

We did have some toys at that time, like *Rock'em Sock'em Robots*, *Electric Football*, and *Incredible Edibles*, but we usually only played with them when the weather was bad. I am from a generation that wanted to spend all day outside with friends instead of playing video games all day in my room.

I was much bigger than Bob, but we wrestled a lot. When we got mad at each other, we'd fight, but we would always make up and keep playing. Sometimes we would take sheets and drape them over the couch and chair like we were in a tent. It was so much fun back then; I wish I still had that imagination. It was like we had no cares or worries in the world. I'm sure both our families had some, but they never let us know about them if they did.

We had a friend, Steven, that lived across the street from me that came over to play with us too. He was older than us, but we didn't care. One day Steven came over and pulled out real bullets. I'd never seen bullets before. I don't know where he got them, but I think he took them from his older brother.

Steven lined up a bunch of bullets through the cracks between the boards on the top of the picnic table, with the bullet part facing down. I was young and didn't know any better, and I guess Steven didn't either because our legs were underneath the picnic table, just sitting there, when Steven took out a hammer and started hitting the top of the bullets. They would make a big noise like a firecracker. He kept going down the line hitting the bullets and making them go off until my mom ran outside after she heard the noise and stopped him. Luckily, none of the bullets hit our legs under the table, but I think we almost gave my mom a heart attack. She called Steven's mom, and I think he got in a lot of trouble.

Bob and I would run to the street when we heard the Ice Cream Man coming and get some kind of wonderful treat. There was one board game I remember playing *Monopoly*. Bob would always beat me. I would get so mad, certain he was cheating, but he was just really smart and knew how to play better than me.

We were best friends for a long time then Bob's family moved away. At the time, I didn't know what that meant, but I was very sad because he wasn't going to be right down the street anymore. The good news was my family moved later, too, and I was a lot closer to Bob again, but that's another story.

PLAYING IN THE CAPITAL

~

Growing up, my dad worked for two different governors. As a result, I spent a lot of time in the capital. My dad would take me to work sometimes on the weekend, and I would just wander around everywhere. Everyone knew who I was and watched out for me while I was adventuring around. I was lucky enough to see the capital from a child's point of view. I would go upstairs to the top of the mezzanine and look down at the big star on the floor below. It looked a long way down, but I was a child, so it probably wasn't as far as it seemed.

I remember going into the House and Senate Chambers and imagining I would work there one day. There is a place where all the past governor's paintings line the walls. I remember going to the center of the capital floor and looking up at the star at the top and walking around looking at their paintings.

My love of history came from the time I spent with my father at his work. I remember my dad's office was on the first floor next to the governor. There were two big doors that I could hardly open by myself. My dad took me to see the governor once, and he gave me a certificate as an Admiral in

Texas Navy. Of course, it was just symbolic because there really wasn't a Texas Navy, but I always thought that was so special. My mom and dad were always invited to fancy parties at the governor's mansion, and sometimes I got to go with them.

One time, I somehow wandered off to one of the "Velvet Rooms" and sat down to eat my finger sandwiches. When my mom found me, she was upset. She told me I wasn't supposed to be in there, but the governor showed up, and he said if I wanted to eat my sandwiches there, to let me. Surprisingly, she did. She was a nervous wreck, thinking that I would drop something and stain that velvet furniture. I didn't.

When Lyndon B. Johnson was elected president of the United States, there was a stage set up on the capital grounds for an event. We were invited to watch from the side of the stage as a famous singer sang to him. There were a lot of people there singing and cheering for him when he spoke.

Not only did my dad work for two governors, but he also wrote some legislation. One Native American Tribe made my dad a lifetime Honorary Chief of their Tribe for one of the bills he wrote for them.

Now that I am older, I see how lucky I was to experience the capital in such a way. It was a fun and educational experience growing up in the capital.

SUMMER MEMORIES

I spent my summers growing up going to my aunt's house in the country. I always went there in the summer to help them with their store and gas station. I used to pump gas, clean windows, fill the windshield wiper tank, check the air in the tires, change tires, fix flats, and stuff like that. This was way before self-service and unleaded gas. Sometimes I would get a nickel or maybe even a dime tip. Most of the time, I just got a smile unless they were grumpy.

I remember there were always some old men in the store telling stories and chewing tobacco. They would spit on the floor. My aunt would get so mad. She would shoo them outside. I didn't know what curse words were back then because my parents never used them, but I'm pretty sure she was using them as they left. The lady in the back at the deli, Aunt Edna, as I called her, made the best bologna sandwiches.

As the years went by, my aunt and uncle had to close the store for some reason. It made me really sad because I loved doing chores there. A couple of times, my best friend, Bob, would come to my aunts with me. We were young; we hadn't lived long enough to be scared of much.

We used to go swimming in my aunt's cow tanks. We would crawl around on our hands and knees, feeling down in the murky bottom for crawfish to use for fishing bait. We went on long excursions in the fields like we were hunters with our BB Guns. We never shot anything but cans on the posts. We weren't very good hunters because we never killed anything and could barely hit the cans unless we were really close.

Growing up in the city, Bob and I didn't know what wonderful experiences we were going to get each summer. They had an old bull, Chester, that we were told to stay away from because he was a little temperamental. We learned the difference between a cow and a bull that summer, as well as life. My uncle would bale hay, and I would help a little bit, so he would pay me a nickel for all my hard work. I remember one time he ended up with a big snake in the hay. This was the first snake I had ever seen.

There was a hat factory in the nearest big town, which really wasn't that big compared to where we lived, where my uncle would always go. Each summer, we would go so he could buy me a straw cowboy hat. Back then, there weren't too many kids with real straw cowboy hats, so I thought that was really cool. After that, he would take me to a little diner and buy me a chicken fried steak. That was the best chicken fried steak I ever had in my life, or maybe it was just because my uncle bought it for me.

One time my uncle took my cousin and me fishing at the bottom land. He dropped us off while he went to check on the cows. Those fish would bite on anything. I think we were the only ones who fished there. We caught so many fish that we put them on a stringer. When our uncle drove up, I pulled the stringer out of the water to show him. There was a big water moccasin with his mouth all the way around one of the fish. We screamed, and I dropped it back in the water fast! My uncle got his rifle, but the snake was gone when I pulled the fish out. A couple of minutes later, we saw that snake swim up to the top of the water. My uncle shot him with one shot. That was the first time I saw anyone shoot a real gun.

I'll never forget all the fond memories and life lessons I learned from those summers.

Taking a Chance

~

After high school, I worked eight to five during the day and went to college from six to ten at night. It was so hard working and going to school all the time while my friends were partying and going places all the time. I kept telling myself I was doing the right thing.

One day a friend of mine told me he could get me a job making a lot of money while building a career. By that time, I was ready to try something else rather than working and going to school all the time, so I took him up on it. I started as an assistant manager for a retail store, making pretty good money for my age plus, it had benefits, like insurance and stock options in the company.

I worked my way up to roving manager. I would run stores while someone was out on vacation or if a full-time manager hadn't been found yet. I loved working there even though the hours were long, and I had to work all the holidays. I was finally able to go out with my friends and do things that I was never able to do since I got out of high school.

While I was working there, I became friends with a band. I watched them perform around town. Those were pretty wild days, and I learned a lot about life and girls.

I met someone at a bar once that led to a really bad relationship. When I finally got myself out of it, I met my special someone, and we were married. One day we reached a point where we were tired of how everything was and the direction our lives were headed. We decided to take a chance and move to another town. We packed up all we had, which wasn't much, and left for the big city.

We didn't have a lot of money when we got there. She got a job waitressing pretty quickly, thankfully. After sleeping in old cheap motels and sleeping in the car, we were finally able to afford a small apartment. After a short time living there, a friend of ours introduced me to a girl he was dating. She had a line on a job in the oil business I could get. After an introduction to one of the managers, I was given the opportunity to work in the oilfield as a consultant.

My father's work had me exploring the capital, but my mother's family worked in the oilfields, so thankfully, I knew something about it. It was a perfect fit for me, and the pay was good. I was able to take care of us after that.

Life was good. Sometimes I think back on how our life may have been had we stayed where we were. The thought is fleeting. Every day I am thankful we took a chance.

THE BLUFFS

When I was a boy, we rode our bikes everywhere. We each had different kinds of bikes, but most of them were Banana Seat Sting Ray types. Some of our friend's dads knew how to weld and made them *Choppers,* which had an extended front tire frame. I think they got it from the movie *Easy Rider* which was popular back then. There were a lot of big hills where we lived that we would pedal up slowly and go down fast. We must have put hundreds of miles on our bikes those years. We didn't just ride on the streets; we rode anywhere we could, sidewalks, dirt paths, up and down driveways. If we could get our bikes on it, we rode on it. One of the places we loved to go ride our bikes we called "The Bluffs."

There were no houses, just dirt hills with paths that had been made from all the kids riding up and down them all the time. There were also ditches you had to pull up on your bike and jump over. I had a bad experience trying to do that one time. All my friends would ride their bikes real fast and pull the front of their bikes up as soon as they reached the top of the hill before the ditch and jump over it. I guess I wasn't very coordinated back then because I didn't know how they did that. They kept telling me it was easy, but I was scared to try it. When they finally convinced me to try, I backed up and started riding as fast as I could, but when I got to the top of the hill where I was supposed to jump over the ditch, I guess I didn't pull up the front of my bike good enough because it went right into the ditch and my face planted right in the ground.

It hurt bad. I ended up with a scrape and bump on my forehead. When I got up, all my friends were laughing at me, but I didn't think it was funny. I was actually crying because I felt weird and couldn't remember things. My best friend started noticing something wasn't right with me. He said for me to follow him to my house. I didn't know what had happened to me, and I couldn't remember how to get home. When we finally got home, we told my mom what had happened. She put a cold rag on my forehead to help me calm down. I guess I had gotten a concussion from hitting my head because the rest of the day, I felt really weird like I was in a fog. My memory started coming back slowly, and eventually, I felt normal again, but there were still some things I don't remember about that day. It was a really scary feeling. I never went back to "The Bluffs" again.

THE CHRISTMAS SQUIRREL

Dedicated to Tammy Koelling –
Words Matter Publishing

It was the night before Christmas, and all through the house, there was something stirring, and it wasn't a mouse!

I kept hearing a really loud noise. What could it be?

It was really quite puzzling to me.

I looked here and there but nothing I could find, and thought that maybe I'm just losing my mind.

Then I saw something move which was very scary as it was pretty big and harry.

I saw it move fast from one place to another, and it looked like it had a long fluffy tail like no other.

I followed it from room to room until it finally stopped.

I found it sitting right on top of a shelf at the very top.

It was upon this very shelf,

I kept my favorite books just for myself.

It looked right at me, and I knew in an instant that it was a rather large squirrel that somehow was existent.

I don't know how it got into my house because it was much larger than a mouse.

I opened the door and tried to coax it onto the floor, but I guess it wasn't ready to leave as he ran from the door.

I used a broom and chased it all around until, in an instant, it couldn't be found.

This squirrel was smart, it waited for me to look away so he could dart.

I finally found it again, and this time out the door, it ran.

I closed the door and took a breath, and said to myself

"What a Christmas Eve it has been with a squirrel upon the shelf!"

On Christmas Day, a new adventure began, as a squirrel once more got in.

I went to take my morning shower, and what should appear, that same squirrel just sitting there!

I had it cornered there when I looked up and saw a small window that was opened just enough to for it to crawl.

I shooed it this way and that, and a little help from my favorite house cat!

When it finally crawled outside, I locked that window up tight in hopes that the squirrel wouldn't come back that night.

I don't know how many people have had a squirrel in their house, but I can tell you they are a lot harder to get out than a mouse.

I thought I was going to be alone this Christmas, but come to find out,

I wasn't alone at all, there's no doubt!

Merry Christmas to all creatures, big and small!

And Happy New Year to you all!

THE GOAT

I grew up loving sports cars. My grandfather used to take me downtown to the old toy store and buy me *Hot Wheels* when I was a kid. I loved them! At Christmas, I would get more and even a racing track to play with them. I would run the tracks all over the house and watch them fly off onto the couch or the floor. I would spend hours doing this until I would finally get tired or it was time to eat. It wasn't just *Hot Wheels* I loved; I also loved model race cars. I would put them together and paint them. At least I tried to; I was still a kid and wasn't very good at it.

When I got a little older, I was a Cub Scout. We had the *Pinewood Derby*, where we would make our own race cars out of a block of wood kit and race them against each other. I remember having a red one that I was really proud of. I ended up taking second place with that car.

From the moment I was old enough to drive, I always wanted a race car. Back then, we called them "Muscle Cars." My first car was an old 1954 Chevy, but it was four doors and not very sporty or very fast. My dad then gave me his old Oldsmobile Delta 88 that had a 455 HP engine, but it wasn't very sporty, either. It would go fast on the highway, but it took a little bit, not that I ever went too fast because my dad would've taken it away from me.

My friends and I would watch the older guys race their cars out at the lake. I always wanted to do that! There were Z-28 Camaros, Chevy Novas, Chevy Chevelle SSs, Ford Boss 429s and Mach 1 Mustangs, Road Runners, Oldsmobile 442s, Dodge Chargers, Pontiac Firebirds, Trans Am 465s, and Pontiac GTOs, as well as many others. My favorite one was the Pontiac GTO, "The Goat."

A guy that lived in our old neighborhood had a 1966 GTO with a Hearse four Speed, positive track rear end, and a Six-Pack with three duces (three two-barrel carburetors). It was black with a wood grain dashboard and a black interior. He kept that car looking like new. I fell in love with it. The day came when he decided to sell it. I was so excited! I asked my dad if he would buy it for me, that I would pay him back. He gave me another life lesson; if there is anything that I really want in life, I need to work for it and save up my money, so that's what I started doing.

I worked hard and saved as much as I could for the day; I was going to buy it. I would ride by the guy's house to make sure it was still for sale. One of my best friends wanted to buy it too, so he asked his dad to buy it and he would pay him back. Unfortunately for me, his dad agreed, and he bought it.

I almost had enough money myself, but I guess it just wasn't meant to be. I never stopped loving that car. My friend let me drive it one time, but it just wasn't the same as it would have been had it been mine. To this day, I would still like to have "The Goat," but they are very rare now and way too expensive just for a dream.

THE HANGING TREE

When I turned sixteen, my grandmother gave me a 1954 Chevrolet that had four doors and a straight six-cylinder motor with three speeds on the column. It had a generator instead of an alternator like cars have today, and the air filter was actually oil in the carburetor cover. The windshield wipers worked with a vacuum, so when you gave the car gas, the windshield wipers would slow down. It was light blue, and I called it the Blue Bomb. I bought a radio and hooked up some speakers in the back with a booster that I could switch on to make the music really loud. All my friends thought that was so cool.

I remember taking my driver's license test at the DPS on my birthday. I did everything perfectly except one small thing. I was driving in a neighborhood when the DPS officer said for me to look at my speed. I glanced down. I was doing twenty-five miles per hour. Not a big deal, but we were in a school zone which meant the speed limit was twenty. That was an automatic failure. I failed because I was going five miles over the speed limit! Five! I was so disappointed. It was my birthday!

How could they fail me on my birthday? They didn't care what day it was. I had screwed up, and they penalized me for it. I was so looking forward to getting my official driver's license. I had to wait until the next day to take the test again, so that night; I was very sad. It was only a day, but it wouldn't be on my birthday.

The first thing the next day, I went back to the DPS to try again. I didn't do nearly as well as I did the first time, but I didn't speed in the school zone again! I learned my lesson. I passed even though I didn't do as well as I had the day before. I was happy and relieved to finally have my official driver's license.

As my luck would have it, my first ticket was for speeding in a school zone. I was embarrassed to tell my mom and dad because they knew why I failed my driver's test the first time, and they no doubt thought I had learned my lesson. I was surprised they weren't mad. They said it was a life lesson; always pay attention and follow all traffic laws to keep me and everyone else safe.

Since I was one of the only one of my friends that had a car, they usually would ride with me everywhere we went. Life was just one long drive with endless music. When you are a teenager, you feel like you're ten feet tall and bulletproof. I don't remember being scared of anything. There was this one time it was getting dark, and my friends wanted to drive out to a house in the country that was supposed to be haunted. We thought we were all grown up and that nothing could scare us. When we got there, some of the guys said they saw a light moving in the old, abandoned house, but I didn't see anything. I think they were just trying to scare everyone.

Across the street from the haunted house was a tree supposedly called the "Hanging Tree". The rumor was that if you drove under the tree and stopped, your car would die. We thought that was just a silly rumor, so I did what any teenager would do. I drove under it. It was just a silly rumor, after all. Believe it or not, my car died! The guys thought I turned it off to scare them, but when they realized that it wouldn't start again, they all started freaking out in fear. We had to get out and push my car from beneath the tree before it would start. That was the weirdest and craziest thing I had ever experienced in my life. Obviously, we never went back there. No one believed us; after all, we were teenagers, and who believes teenagers anyway? The one thing I know is that it really happened, and I will never forget it.

THE MALL

The town I grew up in had very few shops. Convenience stores and a couple of strip malls were all we had to choose from. The town was growing pretty fast. One day someone decided to build a new mall not too far away from where I lived. It took a few years to complete. When they were finished, it was bigger than anything in town. There were all kinds of stores in it. Some I had heard of before and some I never had, so it was really exciting. It was two stories and had an escalator in the middle and stairs on each end. A few of the stores had some cool modern stuff in them. There were also a lot of restaurants with a wide array of food. I remember one restaurant that had a phone in each booth so you could order from your seat. They had the best onion rings I had ever tasted.

There was all kind of clothing stores. I wasn't much into fashion until the mall was built. I began getting clothes that were popular for the time. Had the mall not been built, I don't know that I would ever have cared about what I wore.

It was new and exciting. My friends and I would go all the time. There was this time when my best friend and I went, and we lit a cigarette in the bathroom. We walked down the hall to the mall, smoking like we were all grown up. We felt like we were big guy's until we saw my mom staring right at us. We quickly threw our cigarettes behind our backs and said hi. I don't know if she saw us smoking, but I'm pretty sure there was smoke coming out of our mouths when we said hi. She never said anything, but my friend and I learned a lesson that day. I guess we weren't as grown up as we thought we were. I wonder what our punishment would have been if she did see us and told our dad's?

Through the years, the mall was a safe place to meet up with friends or girls. We never had much money, but we would look at the clothes and shoes and imagine what it would feel like to have them someday. As with a lot of things in life, what was once thriving and full of life is now just an empty space all boarded up. All we have left now are our memories of the times we spent there as children.

THE OILFIELD AND ME

My family has been working in the Texas oilfield since the 1800s. My grandparents had a small house right in the middle of the oilfield. They had a big garden where they raised all their own vegetables and a slaughterhouse where they could process their own meat. During the Great Depression, they raised over thirty children from families that were so poor they just could not take care of them. This was my mom's family, and they had eight children themselves. Life was very hard back then, and they survived by having their own food and working in the oilfield.

As World War I and World War II came and went, they continued making a living there even though all the brothers served in different divisions of the armed service. They were all heroes in their own areas, and thanks to God, they all made it back home safely. The oilfield was very important then and helped provide fuel for our troops. My grandfather was too old for WWII, but he did his part by gathering used tires and things for the war effort. Everyone in the family helped in some way.

I grew up going to the oilfield with my uncles all the time. I watched them drill wells, check the crude oil levels in the tanks, and fix pumps and things all the time. I'll never forget the smell of the oilfield; it wasn't like anything I'd ever smelled before. I always knew when I was getting close to it. Back then, there were no seatbelt laws. I would ride with my uncles all over that oilfield in an old surplus jeep, constantly bouncing around. It was so much fun. Not once did I feel scared about falling out.

The oilfield had been there since the 1800s, and I used to find all kinds of tools and treasures I thought were amazing. All my uncles worked in the oilfield in some capacity, and my aunt was the first "land woman" I had ever heard of. After the war, my uncles built a small submarine and floated in the lake nearby.

I remember seeing pictures of my uncles rotating a well, using mules because it was way before electricity and motorized equipment. My uncles would argue over what the price of oil would get up to one day. One of my uncles said the price of gas would be over $1.00 a gallon some day, but my other uncles thought he was crazy. I wonder what they would think of the current price for a gallon of gas.

The oilfields were very dangerous. I saw some really serious injuries over the years. More than one oilfield worker was missing a finger or two. That was common among the workers. No one in the family ever lost their life, thankfully.

One of my uncles did fall from the top of the bird's nest one time, and fractured his skull. He was in the hospital for a while, but he made it. I think that is the worst injury our family ever had in the oilfield.

It was cool to see a lot of old historical documents and tools in an oil museum in East Texas, that my uncle had donated so everyone could enjoy them.

Some people called the oilfield workers, 'Oilfield Trash." The job is hard and dirty, but they are all some of the most respectable, smart, and generous people I've ever known.

The oilfield is really a small network of people that treat each other like family. We should be thankful for these people. If not for them, we would not have many of the products and luxuries we need, not just for our vehicles but also for our factories and our homes. One thing is for sure; the world would be a much different place without the oilfield and the people who work in it.

THE POOL

I was blessed to grow up in a time when kids could ride their bikes and walk day or night anywhere in the neighborhood, never worrying about someone taking them or hurting them. The only thing we feared was our parents. That is a totally different kind of fear. It seemed like everyone in the neighborhood knew each other's kids and parents. We would ride down to the local park to play basketball, football, or tennis.

One year, they built a neighborhood community pool. Back then, we had to go a long way to go swimming. Very few had their own pool back then. If you paid a small fee, you got a metal tag on a band that you could put around your wrist or arm, or ankle to get access to it. There was a lifeguard, a high and low diving board, an Olympic-style pool, and a kiddy pool for the little kids.

There were a number of older guys who were really good at the diving boards. They would do flips and really cool dives. A few times, they would yell as they jumped, "cannonball" rolled up in a ball or "dingleberry," where they would hold their hands over their privates. Everyone thought that was kind of funny except the lifeguard.

As I grew older, I learned more about girls and really started noticing the difference in their bathing suits. We had many good times at the pool. Summer was spent at the pool, getting an ice cream sandwich or a Dreamsicle from the ice cream machine and a Tahitian Treat drink with extra ice if you wanted it.

After we grew up, many of us left the neighborhood. Eventually, the pool was closed for good. Nowadays, when I see a Dreamsicle or hear the words Tahitian Treat, it takes me back to those summers, back to the joy of being a child with nothing to worry about except the next adventure.

THIRD WHEEL

I was a pretty naive kid growing up. I didn't know much about girls other than they seem to always act silly. I would go to parties with my friends and sometimes we'd go over to one of their houses, and they would go somewhere to "make out" with girls. I was always alone and would end up just listening to music, wishing I was one of them. For some reason, I had girls that were friends, but none of them were ever interested in me. I never understood why. I guess it was because I didn't know what to say to them like my friends obviously did. The girls saw me as more of a brother than a boyfriend.

My friends and I would sneak out of the house we were staying at and go to a girl's house with some of her friends over. They would sneak out and make out with my friends but never with me. Growing up, I was always like a third wheel when it came to girls. I tried a bunch of times to talk to girls and try to get them to want to be with me, but I guess I just didn't know what to say or do back then.

This one time, I really liked this girl, and she seemed to like me a lot too. I brought her flowers and candy for Valentine's

Day. She actually kissed me. I'd never kissed a girl before. I didn't know what I was doing. She kept sticking her tongue in my mouth, but I didn't know what she was doing. She backed up, laughed at me, and left me with the flowers and candy. I was so embarrassed, and felt so stupid! Word got around school really fast about what happened. I was a big football and basketball star, and I didn't even know how to kiss a girl. I wanted the floor to open up and swallow me! When girls walked by me, they would laugh.

One night I was at my best friend's house, and he asked me if I knew how to french kiss. I told him of course I did, I wasn't stupid, but the truth was I didn't have a clue. He said okay, but I don't think he believed me. He still told me what you're supposed to do when you kiss a girl. It may sound unbelievable, but back then, you didn't see such things on TV or anywhere else. You had to learn it on your own. Unfortunately, I never had anyone ever tell me until then. Now I knew how to kiss a girl, but the girls still thought I didn't, so I didn't get to finally kiss one until high school. I wish I had known more about things like that back then, I'm sure my life would have been different, and I would have had a lot more fun.

TRAGEDY IN TEXAS

It was Friday, November 22, 1963; I was six years old. I had been playing outside with my best friend all morning. It was a normal day in our neighborhood. I was starting to get hungry. I went home to see what mom had for lunch when I found her crying in the living room. My best friend's mom was with her, and she was crying too.

"Mom, what's wrong?" I asked.

"Someone shot President Kennedy in Dallas."

My dad worked for Governor John Connally. He was with President Kennedy and got shot too. My heart skipped a beat.

My mom loved President Kennedy. My parents were invited to a dinner for them to meet him, and she was so excited. Unfortunately, the dinner was in Austin after he left Dallas. It was one of the saddest days I remember as a kid, but at the time, I didn't really know or understand what had happened to him. Of course, it was on the TV, and the whole world seemed to be in shock over it. I had never seen my mom or my best friend's mom so upset before. They just couldn't stop crying, and it made me so sad. She was upset over the loss of President Kennedy and Governor Connally being wounded.

As I got older, I understood how tragic it truly was not just for the United States but the world as well. When I was a little older, my mom and dad took me to where President Kennedy got shot in Dallas. I had a sad eerie feeling as I walked behind the grassy knoll and looked down at the street where it happened. I had this feeling that someone bad had stood where I was standing at one time.

I saw some railroad tracks not far away, and I could almost picture someone running over them. I was just a kid and didn't know any real facts about what happened, but I'll never forget the feeling I had standing there like there had been something or someone evil there. I remember going up the staircase and walking by the exact spot where they say the man shot him from. I had that same sad eerie feeling I had behind the grassy knoll.

Governor Connally survived that day, but as everyone knows, President Kennedy didn't. There have been so many conspiracies about what happened that day. I guess we'll never know the truth, but I'll never forget that day and how it affected our family.

One day long after my mom and dad had both gone to Heaven, I was going through one of my dad's old trunks. I found a copy of the speech President Kennedy was going to make at the dinner party in Austin that he never got to make.

I got chills and almost cried when I saw it. It brought back memories of that day. I can't help wondering what the world would be like had the assassination never happened. I'm sure there have been many tragedies in Texas, but the loss of President Kennedy was not only one of the worst, but one of the most historic as well.

TRIP TO MEXICO

Growing up, we took family vacations near and far. We went to the beach or to the mountains and sometimes even to the desert. We saw White Sands, Petrified Wood Forests, the Rocky Mountains, the Grand Canyon, Cactus Forests, Native American villages, and buffalo herds, to name a few. I remember staying in a hotel on the way to see my aunt and uncle in Florida. I watched the Mickey Mouse Show on a black and white TV. When we finally arrived at their house, I ate way too much boiled shrimp.

At the Davis Mountains, I looked in the giant space telescope; the night sky was amazing to behold. Then I took a tour of the underground caves there. During this vacation, my dad's car broke down. I'll never forget the rest of that vacation. We had to stop pretty often because the front hood would pop open. My dad made me get out to close it again over and over. It was almost funny, except that my dad didn't think so after a while.

My dad smoked, and my big sister hated smoke. She would crack her window and stick her nose out to try not to smell it.

One time we went to see our aunt and uncle; they lived on a farm. On our way there, my dad had a wreck on a dirt road. Back then, no one wore seatbelts, and my mom hit her head on the metal dashboard. She had to be taken to the hospital to get stitches. A young cowboy stopped and helped us get out of the ditch. I remember him carrying a gun because he'd been squirrel hunting. My mom was okay and it ended up being a fun trip. We found Native American arrowheads on my aunt and uncle's land. I also, loved wandering around and fishing in their pond too.

One of the places I'll never forget going to was Mexico. My dad loved to go to the greyhound dog races there. We would go over the border to shop, grab something to eat and then go to the dog races. My dad would buy tickets, betting on which dog would win. He kept losing, and finally bought a ticket for every dog racing except one. Guess which one won, of course, it was the only one he didn't buy a ticket for. I don't think he ever went to the dog races again.

When we stopped on the way out of Mexico to eat, some kids told my dad they would watch his car to make sure nothing happened to it for some change. Dad agreed and paid them. When we were through eating, we found that all the hubcaps were gone, and so were the kids; so much for watching the car. My dad was so mad, but there was nothing we could do about it. We never went to Mexico again.

TURK AND STRIKE

Growing up, I thought I had a big backyard to play in. When I got older, I realized that it wasn't as big as I thought. I loved setting traps to try and catch birds. I used an old cardboard box with a stick to hold it up and a long string tied to the stick so I could pull it out when the bird walked under the box to eat the bread I had as bait. I don't know how long I waited, but time seemed to move a lot slower back then. Believe it or not, I actually caught a few, but of course, I let them go, or they flew away.

I remember catching horny toads all the time. It seemed like there were a lot of them back then, but I haven't seen any for a long time. We had a pigeon coup in the back of the yard that my grandfather and uncles built for me. We used to have pigeons. But they all died from something that was in the air. We never got pigeons again. I used to try to catch sparrows that would fly inside it. I caught a few, but I was always gentle and would let them go. I remember we used to have a lot of box turtles that lived in our backyard. I would feed them with lettuce and stuff, but I never kept one as a pet; I wanted them to have the whole backyard to play in.

I don't remember being scared of much back then but, I was scared of yellow jackets because of something that happened at my best friend's house. His big brothers had called me over to look into an old cement mixer next door to their house. They hit it with a brick, and it was full of yellow jackets that flew out and stung me all over my head. I remember running home screaming; it hurt so bad. My mom took me to the doctor. He said I would be alright, but I may be allergic to them from then on. He was right because whenever I got stung after that, wherever I got stung would swell up real big and hurt bad. Even today, I have to have an EpiPen to use if I ever get stung by one.

The only other thing that I remember getting scared of was our next-door neighbors' dogs, Turk and Strike. Turk was an Old English Bulldog, and Strike was the biggest Doberman Pincher I've ever seen. If anyone got near the chainlink fence between our backyard and theirs, they would run into the fence, barking so loud it was scary. I worried that they would go right through that fence one day and get me, but thankfully they never did. Their owner, my neighbor's son, ended up dying in a bad car wreck. I guess they gave his dogs to someone else because I never saw them again. I will never forget Turk and Strike, I guess because I thought they would get me one day.

Another life lesson was learned from Turk and Strike. You may want to watch out for some dogs, as they may not be very friendly.

TWO-A-DAYS

~

I was always running somewhere growing up; I stayed in pretty good shape. When I started playing football, basketball, and track in junior high, I was always doing something. Each sport kept my body in shape in different ways; with football, I had a weight room, and I did a lot of running. In basketball, we did a lot of wind sprints and horses, and in track, we just basically ran all the time. I wanted to stay in shape during the summer while school was out also. I would go to the weight room and run everywhere I went. I wanted to be one of the best players on the team. I knew you had to work hard to be one.

I started in junior high as a defensive end, offensive tight end, and long snapper on punts and extra points. We had a really good team. We beat everyone and won the city football championship. This one time, one of our running backs made a long run for a touchdown, but it was called back because I clipped an opposing player during the run. The vice-principal called me clipper from then on.

Our basketball team was pretty good too. I was taller than most kids my age and had been playing basketball for a long time at the park, so I got to play a lot. I remember one time when we played the faculty in an exhibition game, I had the first jump ball to start the game, and I came right down on our principal's ankle and broke it. Of course, I didn't mean to, but I was known for doing that to the principal the whole time I was there. They even had a picture of him in a cast in the yearbook.

I was a long jumper and a 220/440 distance runner in track. They wanted me to do pole vaulting, high jumping, and hurdling, but I could never get the hang of it. I wasn't coordinated enough for those positions. Track was okay, but I really didn't like it too much. I just played to stay in shape and get a letter for being on a team.

When I got to high school, I found out that football was going to get a lot tougher. They had this thing called "Two-a-Days" at the end of the summer right before school started. The guys trying out for the team would work out two times a day to get in shape for the season. It was hot, and they pushed everyone as far as they could. They would line up long pieces of PVC that they had drilled holes in and attach it to a water hose. When we got a water break, they would give us handfuls of salt tablets, and we would take turns drinking out of the PVC holes.

I'm not sure how any of us survived, but at the end of the second workout, I would pass out when we got home and woke up the next day to do it all over again. As I got older, I got more used to the two-a-days, but they were never easy. One thing is for sure, if you weren't in shape when you started two-a-days, you were before the season started. I'll never forget those days. It helped me to understand that hard work is the key to success.

WHO TOOK THE PICTURES?

We lived in a quiet but normal neighborhood in an average-sized town with a big fenced-in backyard compared to most of our neighbors with plenty of pets running around. One rainy day my sister, brother, and my mom were finally all together in one place after we'd all moved into our own homes. We hadn't been together like this in a long time and were just sitting around talking about some of our fond memories growing up when mom pulled out an old box of pictures from the closet. I didn't even remember seeing them there, but mom knew just where they were. She put the box on the table, and we talked about them as she pulled them out one by one and passed them around.

They were mostly baby pictures of us. We laughed, seeing what we looked like and what we were wearing at different stages of our lives. Most of the pictures were funny; I could remember some of them being taken. There were pictures of holidays, birthdays, and shooting fireworks in the backyard. There were pictures of us through the years. A few had our friends as well as family reunions. Memories of each person who touched my life in some way that led me to the person I am today.

Most of us had forgotten about going to the World's Fair in 1969 in San Antonio until we saw the pictures of the Tower of Americas and the Southwestern Bell Futuristic Pavilion. They had a futuristic push-button telephone that no one had ever seen. We'd only seen rotary dial phones. There was a box you could put food into and cook it really fast, which we know now as a microwave. I remember thinking it was raining and opening my mouth to catch the water. Then I realized that there were no clouds in the sky. Where had the water come from? Someone said the sewer line broke at the top of the tower. Yuck! Another life lesson learned that day. Keep your mouth shut when there are no clouds in the sky.

Some pictures were of us riding our bikes following behind one of those smog trucks that were killing mosquitoes; of course, we didn't know we were probably inhaling DDT. We went from laughing to crying when we came across pictures of our Grandparents who are in Heaven now. After that, we started reflecting on our lives, how much fun we had, and how thankful and blessed, we were. We laughed and cried and hugged. We haven't done that for a long time, but it felt good.

One by one, we talked about our favorites. My mother had us take the ones we wanted. After we picked the ones we wanted, mom put the rest in the box. As we were about to leave, my sister said to mom, "I just realized that dad wasn't in any of the pictures. Where was he?"

Dad had been gone for several years. He is in Heaven with our grandparents now.

Mom smiled, "He was the one who was taking the pictures, Baby."

WHY DO WE HIDE
UNDER OUR DESKS?

~

Elementary school was a whole new experience in my life. My mom took me to the store and bought me all the supplies I would need. On the first day of school, I saw kids I knew from my neighborhood and some I'd never seen before. I learned a lot of lessons there, not just about things they were teaching us but things about life too. One of the lessons was about getting in trouble. One time a girl kept sticking her tongue out at me for some reason, so I stuck mine out back at her. Of course, the teacher saw me. She said that I was being ugly and made me put a bar of soap in my mouth. It made me feel sick to my stomach, but I never stuck my tongue out again.

Another life lesson I learned was about bullies. Some of the bigger guys would pick on the smaller guys. They would make them give them things like their pencils or crayons and sometimes their lunch money. I was bigger than most of the kids, so they didn't bother me too much. I didn't like them being mean to the smaller kids. I also started learning about girls. They were different. They would draw a lot of pictures and pass notes to each other all the time and giggle.

We used to have fire drills every once in a while, where everyone would line up and go outside until the bell rang again. There was also a siren that would make a sound, and we would get under our desks for some reason, sometimes until the teacher said we could come out.

When I got home from school one day, I asked my parents why we had to get under our desks sometimes. They told me one reason was if there was a bad storm or tornado, it could help to protect us. Another thing they tried to explain to me was that a country called Russia didn't like the United States and was always threatening nuclear war. If that happened, they could drop a big bomb on us that could be really bad, and being under the desk could save us. I wasn't sure what either of those things were, but at least I knew there were reasons why.

Third grade was my last at that elementary school. One day at the end of the year, I woke up, and my leg hurt. My dad thought I was just trying to skip school and got mad at me. He drove me to school, but when I got out to go in, I couldn't walk. He took me to the doctor. Come to find out, something had happened inside my leg, and it kept me from being able to walk. I know my dad felt really bad for not believing me because he carried me from the car to the couch inside the house. I could tell he was worried about me, which was very unusual for him because he never showed much emotion or affection. I think it was because he had fought in WWII, and that experience made him pretty tough, so he just didn't show it too often. I ended up never getting to go back to school because I wasn't healed enough yet. I still passed the third grade, and my classmates sent me all kinds of get-well notes and candy. I finally got back to normal, and we moved, so I started going to a new elementary school with new kids and teachers and life lessons.

AUTHOR BIO

Fred Mayfield was born and raised in Texas and lives on five acres there, where he has always loved working on his tractor and taking care of a horse, miniature donkey, goats, parrots, and too many dogs to count. He has spent most of his career in the oilfield as a consultant and in quality management of globally known manufacturers. His expertise has always been in writing procedures and implementing them to improve the quality of products while keeping employees safe. ***Just One Guy's Stories*** is a book that reflects on times that one guy has shared with the world. Everyone has memories of things that happened to them in life, some good and some not so-good. When we reflect on our lives, I believe we all seem to remember the things that made us laugh or cry. Some are silly, and some are sad, but the memories all last a lifetime. As I was writing these stories, I could see myself living through the different experiences in my life and would remember how I actually felt. No matter who you are or where you're from, we all have had similar experiences and stories that we never forget. I hope everyone who reads my stories will reflect on their own lives and what they've experienced. Everyone has stories throughout their lives; I hope you enjoy mine.

"This booklet by Theodore P. Letis formerly titled *A New Hearing for the Authorized Version* is a well thought out synopsis of the Bible translation issue as it keeps before us both the divine and the human aspects in the Bible text debate. This study provides a well-organized approach to understanding how it is possible that an edition of the Bible dating back well over 400 years can be and still is relevant today. Letis has laid out thoughtful stepping stones that link a *theological approach* to Bible translation with the historical understanding of the Bible as a *sacred* text. As one who worked with Dr. Letis on the second edition of this booklet, I highly commend it as edifying to the church. It will prompt a deeper study."

Russell H. Spees, President, Institute for Biblical Textual Studies

"The influence of Theodore Letis' winsome and scholarly defense of the traditional Greek text of the New Testament continues to be felt decades now after his untimely death. In this work, Letis offers a corresponding defense of the Authorized Version, the classic Protestant translation of the Bible in English based upon the Received Text. Its republication in this attractive new edition will serve as a welcomed resource for those who continue to seek out the 'old paths.'"

Dr. Jeffrey T. Riddle (PhD, Union Presbyterian Seminary; MDiv, Southern Baptist Theological Seminary), Pastor of Christ Reformed Baptist Church, Louisa, Virginia

"Learned scholars shine their academic light on the Bible from every angle, but the Bible itself reminds us that 'of the making of many books there is no end' (Ecclesiastes 12:12). This booklet by Theodore Letis wisely ends its survey of learned scholars and their opinions by setting before our consciences this vital truth: The Bible is the only book that leads us to heaven. We should love, learn, and be devoted to the Authorized Version of God's inspired Word."

Maurice Roberts, Retired Editor, *The Banner of Truth Magazine*

"'So then faith cometh by hearing, and hearing by the word of God' (Romans 10:17). *Today's Christian & the Church's Bible* upholds the AV/KJV as the Word of God due to its superior underlying text (the Ecclesiastical Text) and method of translation (Formal Equivalency) which is in keeping with the verbal and plenary inspiration and preservation of the Holy Scriptures. This primer is worth your time and attention. *Tolle Lege.*"

Rev. Dr. Jeffrey Khoo (BTh, MDiv, STM, PhD),
Principal, Far Eastern Bible College, Singapore

"This booklet, in its original printing as *A New Hearing for the Authorized Version*, opened my eyes to solid reasons of principle for the use of the AV and the rejection of the modern translations, which use the older Greek mss. I recommend it to all who view being faithful to the inspired Scripture as important."

David J. Engelsma, Emeritus Professor, Protestant Reformed Seminary, Grand Rapids, Michigan

Today's Christian &
the Church's Bible

TODAY'S
CHRISTIAN
-&-
THE
CHURCH'S
BIBLE

A Time to Return to the
Authorized Version

Theodore P. Letis, PhD

Kept Pure Press

Today's Christian & the Church's Bible: A Time to Return to the Authorized Version
by Theodore P. Letis

Originally published as *A New Hearing for the Authorized Version* in 1978 by
Theodore P. Letis.

Re-published in 1997 by The Institute for Renaissance
and Reformation Studies

This edition first published July 2023
© 2023 Kept Pure Press LLC

This edition was edited and updated by Christian M. McShaffrey,
editor-in-chief of the *Text & Translation* webzine, and owner
of Kept Pure Press with the kind permission of Dr. Letis' family.

All scripture references are taken from the
Authorized (King James) Version of the Bible.

Font(s): Amster, Cardo, Kings Caslon, MrsEavesPetiteCaps, Vollkorn.

Made in the United States of America

Library of Congress Control Number: 2023909319

ISBN (paperback): 978-1-953855-53-4
ISBN (PDF): 978-1-961495-00-5
ISBN (EPUB): 978-1-953855-77-0

1 2 3 4 5 6 7 8 9 10   27 26 25 24 23

KEPT PURE

IN ALL AGES

Learn more about the traditional text of the Bible:
textandtranslation.org

Contents

- Introduction -

Modern man is a manipulated creature. The merchandisers of the world have conditioned him to believe that he must have variety and multiple choice for everything from toothpaste to gravestones.

He has reached the point that if he does not have several options to choose from he feels forced upon by some authority other than his own freedom of choice. No dimension of life is sacrosanct, including religion.

Not only do we have a religion (or denomination) for every conceivable disposition, but now we have Bibles to suit any temperament. If you have not seen one that you like yet, wait awhile; it will arrive. I find that I can tolerate most of this multiplicity of variety except when it comes to the Bible, and that is because I cannot seem to make it all fit with my idea of a "final authority" (for all matters of faith and practice). Perhaps my problem is that I take the issue too seriously.

Nevertheless, I have made a comparison of the English Bibles published from 1525 (Tyndale's) to the present, 1978 (New International Version, first edition), with a view to the New Testament specifically, and have arrived at the following conclusion:

Keeping in consideration both the divine and the human aspects of the Bible, the Authorized Version (which shall hereafter be referred to as AV or King James Version) should be retained in the churches, in Bible studies, and in the classroom, because of the superiority of its Greek text, translation, and English usage; and because it is a link with our past as well as a unifying factor for the present.

Keeping in mind both the human and the divine aspects of the Bible the first area we will examine is that of the Greek text.

ONE

– *The Scrolls and the Parchments* –

One of the most prevailing criticisms of the AV is that it was produced before we had the advantage of recent manuscript discoveries.[1] For example, it was not until the late nineteenth century that scholars took full advantage of two of the oldest New Testament manuscripts, Codices Vaticanus and Sinaiticus, both of the fourth century.[2]

In spite of the antiquity of these two documents, however, some scholars believe they are edited copies because they differ from the majority of the rest of the manuscripts.

Moreover, they differ from one another in over 3,000 places in the gospels alone.[3] John William Burgon, a scholar who personally examined these two "old" documents, characterized them as follows:

We suspect that these two Manuscripts are indebted for their preservation, *solely to their ascertained evil character;* which has occasioned that the one eventually found its way, four centuries ago, to a forgotten shelf in the Vatican library: while the other, after exercising the ingenuity of several generations of critical Correctors, eventually (viz. in A.D. 1844) got deposited in the waste-paper basket of the Convent at the foot of Mount Sinai. Had B and א been copies of average purity, they must long since have shared the inevitable fate of books which are freely used and highly prized; namely, they would have fallen into decadence and disappeared from sight. But in the meantime, behold, their very Antiquity has come to be reckoned to their advantage.[4]

Burgon had good reason for doubting the reliability of Vaticanus and Sinaiticus, if only because they differed so radically from the majority of the manuscripts. It was on the majority that the AV was based, which thus assured it of the greatest possible accuracy, until the discovery of Vaticanus and Sinaiticus.

In what ways do these two ancient documents differ from the majority? It can be summed up in one word: omissions—close to five thousand altogether.[5] Although it has been continuously asserted that none of these omissions (and other alterations) affect doctrine, the following examples seem to indicate otherwise:

1 Timothy 3:16
The *Authorized Version* reads:
". . . *God* was manifest in the flesh."
Sinaiticus (*Vaticanus* is missing this portion) reads:
". . . Who was manifest in the flesh."

Colossians 1:14
The *Authorized Version* reads:
"In whom we have redemption *through his blood*, even the forgiveness of sins."
Vaticanus and *Sinaiticus* read:
"In whom we have redemption, even the forgiveness of sins" ("*through his blood*" omitted).

Luke 2:33

The *Authorized Version* reads:

"And *Joseph* and his mother marveled."

Vaticanus and *Sinaiticus* read:

"And his *father* and his mother . . ."

This latter variant is of no small significance in light of a book titled *The Illegitimacy of Jesus: A Feminist Theological Interpretation of the Infancy Narratives* (1987). Here, Professor Schaberg argues that Jesus was, as the title of her book makes clear, illegitimately born to Mary and Joseph and that it was Luke's intention to demonstrate that "This child will be holy because the Holy Spirit will come upon his mother, and she will experience divine protection and empowerment even in a situation deemed unholy."[6] Moreover,

> The process of gradual Christian erasure of the tradition [of Jesus' illegitimacy] began here in the gospels, as the evangelists attempted to minimize the potential damage of the tradition and maximize its power. The tradition became

a subtext, difficult to read.[7]

In other words, later Christians altered this truth of Jesus' illegitimacy by turning it into a virginal birth, but the earlier manuscripts, such as Codices *Vaticanus, Sinaiticus* (and *Bezae*), which read *his father and his mother*, still suggest remnants of the original tradition. We can see here how such small alterations in the text can have profound implications for theology.

Some of the other lengthy passages omitted by these documents are as follows:

John 7:53-8:11

The entire account of the woman taken in adultery, 12 verses in all.

John 5:3-4

The account of the angel troubling the water.

Mark 16:9-20

Twelve verses in all recounting the resurrection and the ascension.

It will be asked why are these manuscripts so highly regarded if they lack so much that has been traditionally regarded as Scripture?

Most scholars will answer that antiquity must be regarded as the highest priority.[8]

In effect, the criterion of *antiquity* alone has prevailed over the *majority*, and today all modern versions from 1881 on (with the rare exception of *The 21st Century King James Version*, which I shall address shortly), either are based on, or have reference to, these two manuscripts (and some kindred papyri), even though they seriously conflict with the majority, and each other.

Dean Burgon (1883) had the following to say concerning the advocates of this new textual theory:

> They [Westcott and Hort] exalt B [*Vaticanus*] and Aleph [*Sinaiticus*] . . . because in their own opinions those copies are the best. They weave ingenious webs, and invent subtle theories, because their paradox of a few against the many requires ingenuity and subtlety for its support.[9]

There were other men along with Burgon who never lost sight of the divine aspect of the book and who realized that, though an open mind should be kept with regard to new manuscript discoveries, they were not ready to "take away from the words of the book" so quickly. They wanted to wait until all the evidence was in. There were others who wanted the Bible updated immediately according to the findings. Two such men were Bishop B. F. Westcott and F. J. A. Hort.

Endnotes Chapter One

1 American Bible Society, *Why So Many Bibles?* (New York: American Bible Society, 1968), p. 5.

2 *Ibid.*, p. 15.

3 H. C. Hoskier's *Codex B and Its Allies: A Study and an Indictment*, vol. I (London: Bernard Quaritch, 1914), p. vi.

4 John W. Burgon, *The Revision Revised*, 2nd ed. (London: John Murray, 1885), p. 319.

5 Wilbur N. Pickering, *The Identity of the New Testament Text* (Nashville: Thomas Nelson Inc., 1977), p. 16.

6 Jane Schaberg, *The Illegitimacy of Jesus: A Feminist Theological Interpretation of the Infancy Nawrratives* (San Francisco: Harper and Row Publishers, 1987), p. 125.

7 *Ibid.*, p. 195.

8 Sir Fredric Kenyon, *Our Bible and the Ancient Manuscripts*, 5th ed. (London: Eyre & Spottiswoode, 1958), p. 3.

9 W. MacLean, *The Providential Preservation of the Greek Text of the New Testament*, 3rd ed. (Gisborne, NX: Westminster Standard Publications, 1977), p. 11.

TWO

– *The Revised Version of 1881-83* –

Westcott and Hort were the leading force on a revision committee formed in 1879 to update the AV by ridding it of obsolete words and by correcting "plain and clear errors."[1] In fact, they were given eight general rules to follow, one of which was "to introduce as few alterations as possible into the text of the AV consistently with faithfulness."[2]

This principle, however, was stretched to its limit— some would say it was actually violated-when the revised Greek text Westcott and Hort had been conjointly constructing for nearly twenty years was introduced to the revision committee, a section at a time. It was a text revised to the standard of Vaticanus and Sinaiticus.

Burgon, who had not been invited to work on the

committee and so had some degree of detachment, had a few words to say about this switching of Greek texts which has subsequently affected nearly every translation to date:

> Shame, — yes, *shame* on that two-thirds majority of well-intentioned but most incompetent men who, — finding themselves (in an evil hour) appointed to correct "*plain and clear errors*" in the *English* "Authorized Version," — occupied themselves instead with *falsifying the inspired Greek Text* in countless places, and branding with suspicion some of the most precious utterances of the Spirit! Shame, yes, *shame* upon them![3]

Westcott and Hort's type of Greek text has prevailed in Bible translation work to the present day. Since their time, however, we have had an opportunity to take a closer look at the materials at hand; and as a result, some scholars are now starting to return to the type of Greek text on which the AV was based.[4]

Endnotes Chapter Two

1 F. F. Bruce, *The English Bible*, 2nd ed. (New York: Oxford University Press, 1970), p. 139

2 *Ibid.*, p. 137

3 John Burgon, *Revision Revised*, p. 135

4 On this point consult H. C. Hoskier's *Codex B and Its Allies: A Study and an Indictment*, 2 vols. (London: Bernard Quaritch, 1914), wherein he has a dedication which reads as follows: "This essay is respectfully dedicated to the next body of revisers in the hope that it may prove of some service to them." In the wake of this seminal work see more recently, Wilbur N. Pickering, *The Identity of the New Testament Text* (Nashville: Thomas Nelson Inc., 1977); Jakob Van Bruggen, *The Ancient Text of the New Testament* (Winnipeg: Premier Printing, 1976); Brevard Childs, *The New Testament as Canon* (Philadelphia: Fortress Press, 1984), *Excursus I*, pp. 518-530; and my own *The Ecclesiastical Text: Text Criticism, Biblical Authority and the Popular Mind* (Institute for Renaissance and Reformation Biblical Studies, 1997).

THREE

- *Biblical English* -

With regard to English usage, the AV has been both praised and scorned; praised for the power and beauty of its language; scorned because that language is regarded as "archaic." The best defense for the language of the AV, however, is a professional appraisal of the state of today's English, and for that we turn to remarks made by George Orwell:

> Most people who bother with the matter at all would admit that the English language is in a bad way, but it is generally assumed that we cannot by conscious action do anything about it . . . [B] ut an effect can become a cause, reinforcing the original cause and producing the same effect

in an intensified form, and so on indefinitely . . . [I]t is rather the same thing that is happening to the English language. It becomes ugly and inaccurate because our thoughts are foolish, but the slovenliness of our language makes it easier for us to have foolish thoughts.[1]

Americans are particularly susceptible to this criticism because of the ubiquitous influences of consumerist slogans and the national past-time of creating jargon and euphemisms in the business world and in popular journalism.

What might this say for the argument that the Scriptures, with their regal thoughts and concepts, should be wrestled down from heavenly plateaus and made to speak through a language that is "ugly and inaccurate"? What would the effects be on those concepts as a result? Perhaps Kenneth Taylor's *Living Bible* will serve as a fair example:

I Samuel 20:30

"You son of a bitch!"[2]

I Kings 18:27

"Perhaps he is talking to someone or else is out sitting on the toilet."

Should we not want to infuse contemporary English with a slightly higher form of expression, such as is found in the AV? Pierson Parker noted in his insightful essay, "In Praise of 1611," that,

> It may well be that the flaccidity and banality of much twentieth-century English stems from the fact that people today do not know the Bible, the 1611 Bible, as their forefathers did. Yet we long for a fuller command of English among college and university graduates.[3]

Some will reply, "that is an artificial approach; no one can be expected to go backward; besides, when the Bible was originally written it was in the language of the day." Woodrow W. Hill would reply,

While the original language of the New

Testament was conversational in nature, the truths communicated were elevated and spiritual. For this reason it seems inappropriate to many for the vehicle used in conveying these sacred truths to have too much of the smell of the mundane upon it.[4]

I hear someone else responding with "Yes, but even the AV was in contemporary language in its day!" This is another of those popular misconceptions, I'm sorry to say, used by modern Bible publishers to legitimize whatever version they are pushing onto the market. According to Dr. Edward F. Hills, an authority on the AV:

The English of the King James Version is not the English of the early 17th century. To be exact, it is not a type of English that was ever spoken anywhere. It is Biblical English, which was not used on ordinary occasions even by the translators who produced the King James Version. As H. Wheeler Robinson (1940) pointed out, one need only compare the preface written by the translators with the text of their translation to feel the difference in style.... The King James Version... owes its merit not to 17th century English—which was very different— but to its faithful translation of the original... its style is that of the Hebrew and of the New Testament Greek.[5]

To me that seems to say that the AV is in one sense timeless, and as such, cannot be rightly called archaic. One last response, however, to the sincere advocates of "the Bible in the language of the people":

Again it is sheer accident, and wholly artificial, that Elizabethan language should be associated in the public mind with worship—just as it is accident and artifice that make us think 'church' when we see gothic architecture. But legitimate or not, the association has been made and is a fact of our life. Even the RSV and NEB translators, when they come to hymns and prayers, revert to the 'Thee's' and 'Thou's' of yester-century.

The question is by no means frivolous: if, as RSV and NEB testify, the tongue of Elizabeth is proper for hymns and prayers, why is it not proper for all Scripture reading in the churches?[6]

As for the overall difficulty of Elizabethan English, this is also a popular fallacy born of a scornful age. Dr. Rudolf Flesch, one of the leading authorities on readable writing, has shown that the difficulty of any reading material can be gauged by the number of affixes per hundred words. For example,

> The average reader standard of 37 is important to know. The best example of very easy prose (about 20 affixes per 100 words) is the King James Version of the Bible: literary writing tends to be fairly difficult; scientific prose is very difficult. This book has on the average per 100 words, 33 affixes.[7]

Incidentally, a good example of a modern Bible that tends to be "difficult" for the average reader is the *New*

English Bible (1961-70). Terence H. Brown noted that:

> In many places the homely Anglo-Saxon words
> [in the KJV] have been displaced by stilted
> Latinisms, and simple expressions exchanged
> for more difficult ones. Typical examples
> are: machinations (lying in wait), anxious to
> ingratiate (willing to do the Jews' pleasure),
> beneficent work (grace), indefatigable in
> confuting (mightily convinced), arrogates
> (takes), inscribed (written), extirpate (destroy).
> Outstanding examples of pompous pedantry
> are to be found in I Tim. 4:3 'inculcating
> abstinence'; I Tim. 6:4 'pompous ignoramus';
> James 3:8 'intractable evil.'[8]

It appears that the popular notions that the AV is
difficult because it is, while modern versions tend to be
easy because they are contemporary, are both fallacious.

Endnotes Chapter Three

1 George Orwell, "Politics and the English Language," in *Readings For Writers*, ed. JoRay McCuen and Anthony C. Winkler (New York: Harcourt Brace Jovanovich, Inc., 1977), p. 299.

2 This was actually altered in later editions because of the storm of protest it precipitated.

3 Pierson Parker, "In Praise of 1611," *Anglican Theological Review* 3 (July 1964), pp. 251-60.

4 Broadman Press, *What Bible Can You Trust?* (Nashville: Broadman Press, 1974), pp. 99-100. Moreover, it would seem that even the well repeated slogan that the New Testament was written in "street language" has been called into question since the days of Deissmann (1866-1937), who first popularized this notion, as we will see under sections dealing with translation philosophy, "utilitarian" and "theological."

5 Edward F. Hills, *The King James Version Defended*, 4th ed. (Des Moines: The Christian Research Press, 1973), p. 218.

6 Pierson Parker, "In Praise of 1611," pp. 251-60.

7 Rudolf Flesch, *The Art of Plain Talk* (New York: Harper & Brothers Publisher, 1946), p. 43.

8 Terence H. Brown, *The New English Bible* 1961-1970 (London: The Trinitarian Bible Society, 1970), pp. 1-2.

FOUR

– *Thees and Thous* –

The issue of specific archaisms in the AV is one that has been abundantly over-labored but should be addressed. Though more may exist, Hills offers only seventeen serious examples of words which have changed meaning since 1611.[1]

Nevertheless, almost every modern version justifies its existence on the basis of these archaisms; and certainly it must be admitted that there is something to be said for updating obsolete words. Why is it, though, that we do not feel such a compulsion with regard to Shakespeare's works? The answer is probably that while all should be literate in Shakespeare, there are probably many who never will be.

Holy Scripture should be made as accessible as

possible, to all levels of literacy. Hence, the appearance of a masterful updated edition of the classic AV now allows anyone with a desire to use the old Anglican Bible to do so, less the archaisms.

The 21st Century King James Version is an exact reproduction of the AV with accurate, modern equivalents for all the several archaisms found throughout its last revision.[2] The complaint of difficult archaisms is no longer available for those who want to impatiently dismiss this sacred classic.

Moreover, there is actually an advantage to the antiquated pronouns that modern translation advocates are either uninformed about, or else rather quiet regarding.

Late in the twentieth century, Thomas Nelson, knowing a market when they saw one, made an attempt to update the old workhorse of both high church liturgists, as well as low church fundamentalists, but also gave way like the *Revised Version* before it, this time in the Old Testament text, and by ditching the Tyndalian/ Elizabethan second person singular/plural distinctions (i.e., the thees and thous) in their "New" *New King James Bible*.

Dr. Mikre-Sellassie, a United Bible Societies translation consultant, rehearsed in an article he wrote for *The Bible Translator* in April of 1988 (pp. 230 -237), why the "thees" and "thous" cannot be dispensed with in good conscience.

While many marketing-types think these terms are the shibboleth by which consumers will judge whether a Bible is "modern" or not (while trying to make up their minds at the shelf of their local religious bookstore), it is no justification for erasing the important grammatical function these terms actually fulfill. I shall let him speak in his own voice:

Translators, and especially those in common language projects, may find it strange and surprising to hear a consultant recommending use of the King James Version for translation . . . . The archaic English pronouns of the KJV distinguish number in the second person pronoun in all cases, as shown in [the accompanying] table. Thus the KJV can certainly render an important service to those translators who do not have any knowledge of the source languages of the Bible and therefore work only from an English base, in easily distinguishing between "you singular" and "you plural."[3]

Hence, it is impossible to communicate this important grammatical point without Elizabethan/Biblical English terms, as found in the AV and as retained in the KJ21.

	SINGULAR			**PLURAL**
1st Person	I			we
2nd Person	thou/thee/thy/thine			ye/you/your
	Masculine	Feminine	Neuter	
3rd Person	He	She	It	they

Endnotes Chapter Four

1   Hills, *The King James Version*, pp. 217-218.

2   *The 21st Century King James Version* (Gary, South Dakota: 21st Century King James Bible Publishers, 1994).

3   Ammanuel Mikre-Sellassie, "Problems in Translating Pronouns From English Versions," *The Bible Translator* vol. 39 (April 1988): pp. 230-237.

FIVE

– The "Language of the People"? –

We will now illustrate the fragmentation that has occurred as a result of so many "Bibles in the language of the people," vying to replace the AV and thus assume the monopoly of which it alone could once boast.

Hopefully, this will also demonstrate the fallacy of trying to ascertain just what is the "language of the people."

The following quotations are from the book *What Bible Can You Trust?*, which supplies a brief description of the purpose for which several of the more important modern Bibles have been published. Though most of them give more reasons, all of them give the following:

The New Testament in Modern Speech, Weymouth, 1903:

"To consider how it could be most accurately and naturally exhibited in the English of the present day."[1]

Centenary Translation of the N.T., Montgomery, 1924:

". . . to make a translation chiefly designed for the ordinary reader . . . . "[2]

The Bible: A New Translation, Moffatt, 1926:

"The aim I have endeavoured to keep before my mind in making this translation has been to present the books... in effective, intelligible English . . ."[3]

The New Testament, An American Translation, Goodspeed, 1923:

" . . . those facts were adequate reasons for a new translation . . . put in the familiar language of today."[4]

The New Testament in the Language of the People, Charlie Williams, 1937:

"Dr. Williams . . . felt a need to produce a translation which would be as understandable to modern English readers as the original Greek text was to the reader of the first century."[5]

Revised Standard Version, 1952:

"A common slogan associated with the first publicity was: the Word of Life in Living Language."[6]

Today's English Version, 1966:

"This translation . . . came in response to repeated proposals that a translation be made that would be understood by anyone who reads English . . ."[7]

The New English Bible, 1970:

"We aim at a version which shall be as

intelligible to contemporary readers as the
original . . . ."[8]

New American Standard Version, 1971:
". . . to make the translation in a fluent and
readable style according to current English
usage."[9]

**The Living Bible Paraphrased,
Ken Taylor, 1971:**
"Ken Taylor has . . . made the Bible readable."[10]

The New International Version, 1973:
"Opinions were garnered from men of wide
and diverse theological and denominational
backgrounds. The consensus was that, in spite
of the fine features of many translations, there
was a need for an up-to-date
translation [!] . . . ."[11]

Let us at this point invoke a little common sense and
logic into the discussion. These, of course, are only a few

of the major versions, but the reader is left with one of three conclusions after reading the *raison d' être* for each of these modern editions:

(1) all previous attempts at putting the Bible into the language of the people have failed, thus prompting continuous attempts;

(2) our language has been changing so fast that we need a new translation every few years to keep up with it; or

(3) there are *other* factors that prompt one to make a translation of the Bible, which, when discovered, will explain why we have become inundated with modern Bibles.

Once one gets free of advertising slogans, two factors suddenly materialize offering insight as to what has prompted such a torrent of Bibles "in the language of the people": first, a low regard for Scripture as a sacred text; and second, the economic determinism that governs free enterprise, which then enters to exploit the first point.

Concerning the first point, we refer to C. S. Lewis'

work *The Literary Impact of the Authorized Version*, in which he demonstrates that the movement to regard the Bible "as literature" arose from the era of Romanticism, the result of which negated any view of the Bible as a sacred text. It was this prevailing view of "the Bible as literature" that led some to try their hand at rendering a new translation "in the language of the people," thus assuring for themselves a sort of immortality through their work.

The second factor, that of economic determinism, is probably the more significant of the two considerations. Paul told Timothy "The love of money" was the root of all evil, and I suppose Marx had a better grasp of this truth than most Christians have.

Unfortunate as it may be, the economic factor is a strong incentive to any publisher to consider the guaranteed returns of publishing a Bible.

It is common knowledge that since the invention of printing, the Bible has virtually dominated the field as the best seller of all time. Cunniff, an Associated Press business analyst put it this way:

In the cold, hard, material world of book selling, there is nothing like the Bible. The Word sells like nothing else. It beats sex, diet, money, and fad books. It has no equal year after year.[12]

It can almost be predicted that, just by publishing a "*New* Bible" and getting some well-known evangelical or academic to endorse it, one will insure a considerable profit.

A case in point is Ken Taylor's *Living Bible*. Since the publication of this paraphrased version, as early as 1976 Taylor had sold well over twenty-three million copies and formed his own major publishing company (Tyndale House Publishing).[13]

Further examples could be shown, such as the economic success story of a small regional religious publisher, Zondervan. Soon after publishing the *New International Version*, it became a part of the massive conglomerate owned by Rupert Murdoch, of which Harper and Row, and Collins are just a part.[14]

Enough has been established, however, to make clear that these two factors, the Bible treated as literature, and economic considerations, will insure that there will be no end to new "Bibles in the language of the people."

Endnotes Chapter Five

1 Broadman Press, *What Bible*, p. 39.

2 *Ibid.*, p. 40.

3 *Ibid.*, p. 41.

4 *Ibid.*, p. 42.

5 *Ibid.*, p. 43.

6 *Ibid.*, p. 48.

7 *Ibid.*, p. 65.

8 *Ibid.*, p. 70.

9 *Ibid.*, p. 76.

10 *Ibid.*, p. 81.

11 *Ibid.*, p. 84.

12 John Cunniff, Associated Press Release: "Bible Still the Best Seller," 1976.

13 *Ibid.*

14 For just a glimpse of Murdoch's power as a media mogul, see Henry Porter's interesting analysis, "The Keeper of the Global Gate," *The Guardian* Tuesday, 29 October 1996, pp. 2-5.

SIX

– Historical Ethos:
The Forgotten Factor –

Concerning translation, it seems the AV has had more than its share of criticism. It has become fair game, and open season declared, for every first-year Greek student to display his command of Greek grammar by pointing out so-called "inaccurate translations" in the AV.

I suppose this is to be anticipated since the temptation to correct a 400 year-old document must be more than some can resist. There is, however, a quaint anecdote that illustrates the truth that "a little learning is a dangerous thing."

Dr. Kilbye, on one of the translating committees for the AV, went to a Sunday morning service and heard a young preacher waste a great amount of his sermon time criticizing several words in the then-recent translation.

The preacher meticulously illustrated with three reasons why he felt a particular Greek word should have been rendered differently.

Later that evening, the preacher and Dr. Kilbye, who were strangers, were invited together to a meal. Dr. Kilbye took this opportunity to tell the preacher that he could have used his time more profitably. He then explained how the translators had very carefully considered the "three reasons" given in the sermon, but were constrained by thirteen more weighty reasons for translating the word the way they did.

This is a good opportunity to point out that in the seventeenth century, scholarship had reached no mean attainment.

Lancelot Andrews, one of the translators (at home in fifteen modern languages, not to mention his command of Latin, Greek, Hebrew, Chaldee, Syriac, and Arabic), spent the greater part of five hours a day in prayer.

John Boys, another on the translating committee, spent sixteen hours a day studying Greek. It must be remembered, there were not the enemies of learning to contend with in those days, such as television, radio, telephone, internet, or jet travel for trips to the Holy Land. All spare time for these men was consumed with learning.

John Alfred Faulkner noted that these translators also, "had a deeply religious spirit which was thoroughly in rapport with the sacred text, and could therefore reproduce in print its wonderful spiritual atmosphere."[1]

The unique historical and cultural setting that gave birth to this translation, when compared with the technocratic-secularism of much of modern western culture, is a consideration which must not be lightly dismissed as incidental. Again, Faulkner observes:

> In 1611 the civilization of England was saturated with religion, not with science. Everybody thought and talked theology. 'Theology rules there' wrote Grotius of England in 1613. Religion and culture were then firm friends . . . The whole moral effect which is produced nowadays by religious newspaper, tract, essay, lecture, missionary report, sermon, was then produced by the Bible alone.[2]

I am not, of course, arguing from these facts that the AV could never be improved in all of its translation.[3] Rather, my point is that we should not think for a moment that the twentieth century has the advantage of some special insight into linguistics because of its modern technological context.[4] Modern does not always equal better.

In his article, "In Praise of 1611," mentioned earlier, Pierson Parker has brought to light the enduring quality of the translation work behind the AV. He has found no less than forty-four instances where the AV has a superior translation as compared to the *Revised Standard Version*, in the books of First Corinthians, Second Corinthians, and Galatians.

After giving these examples, he concluded his article on a slightly ironic note (ironic in that Parker is one of the leading lights in the areas of source criticism and the synoptic problem):

> So my conscience troubles me, a little, now and then . . . . I have seldom used the KJV in book, article, lecture, or seminar — except,

occasionally, to point out its shortcomings. Shortcomings, it certainly has. But then, one of life's easiest tasks is to find deficiencies in the work of other men. The KJV has, likewise, its own gigantic strength — strength which no amount of tinkering could reproduce in the RSV or the ARV or the NEB. Perhaps while retaining those others, I ought to expose my students more fully to the work of 1611. For they will find here a Bible that is rich, rewarding, and sometimes, even right.[5]

Endnotes Chapter Six

1 John Alfred Faulkner, "English Bible Translations," *Biblical Review Quarterly* (April 1924): pp. 199-231.

2 *Ibid.*

3 It appears that at least at one point the translators retained a creative, proto-dynamic equivalent translation left over from Tyndale's edition, e.g. "Easter" for the Greek "πασχα," Acts 12:4. On this see the helpful treatment found in the *Quarterly Review* 470 (January-March 1980): pp. 15-16.

4 There has been much published in recent days concerning the value of the Egyptian papyri discoveries and the insights they provide for the New Testament vocabulary and usage. Nevertheless, theologically speaking, in that the Biblical usage of the Greek language was a vehicle to convey inspired Revelation, as opposed to the secular usage of the papyri, the Scriptures themselves should always be consulted as a more reliable source for determining "revelational" meaning and usage. The Greek grammarian Nigel Turner has made a special contribution in this area, and as F. F. Bruce put it so succinctly, "As long as scriptural writers hug the coast of mundane affairs, the Egyptian pharos yields a measure of illumination to their tract; but when they launch out into the deeps of divine counsels, we no longer profit by its twinkling cross-lights" F. F. Bruce, *The Books and the Parchments*, 1950, p. 64.

5 Parker, "In Praise of 1611, " p. 260.

SEVEN

– The Modern Approach to Translation (Utilitarian) –

James Moffatt, one of the earliest to offer his own modern twentieth-century translation of the Bible, wrote in the preface to his edition in 1913: "Once the translation of the New Testament is freed from the influence of the theory of verbal inspiration... difficulties cease to be so formidable." Theologically, however, difficulties may just begin.

The prevailing modern philosophy of Bible translation now being used by the American Bible Society is called the "dynamic-equivalence" method and has been borrowed from modern communications theory. Several scholars such as James Daane,[1] Noel K. Weeks,[2] and Jakob Van Bruggen,[3] have noted the loss of original Biblical content in the translations produced by this method.

Simply stated, those who advocate this theory maintain that "communicating" is the all-consuming priority — as a result, the Biblical content must be reduced to the receptor language categories, thought forms, and cultural points of reference, for real communication to take place.

This may sound like a reasonable approach to translation until it is discovered that one's theology will color the determination of what should be regarded as "essential," and therefore what should be translated literally, and that which is "non-essential," and should be translated in such a manner as would be understood in the receptor language, even if the original content must be altered.

E. A. Nida, the American Bible Society's former Executive Secretary for Translations and the major proponent of the dynamic-equivalence theory, gives an example showing why a major tenet — perhaps its very foundation — of historic Christianity, such as the dogma of the substitutionary atonement of Christ, should be exchanged for a concept that would be more readily understood in a given culture:

> One of the most common interpretations of
> the atonement has been substitutionary, in
> the sense that Christ took upon Himself our
> sins and died in our place as a substitutive
> sacrifice. This interpretation, true and valuable
> as it may be for many, is not communicable
> to many persons today, for they simply do not
> think in such categories . . . [T]he presentation
> of the Atonement in terms of reconciliation is
> more meaningful, since in this way they can
> understand more readily how God could be in
> Christ reconciling the world to Himself.[4]

The problem that Noel Weeks sees with this
reductionism is that, "the original Scripture was not
written on this assumption."[5]

Weeks feels that turning the Biblical text into an
evangelistic tract so that it will be comprehensible to
the unbeliever (who it might be expected would not
readily understand the theology of the substitutionary

atonement, even in the post-Christian West, or other important Christian distinctives), is "turning Scripture to a use for which it was not originally designed."[6]

This is not, however, a remote problem dealing only with missionary translation work, but has been used in producing the *Today's English Version (Good News for Modern Man)*.

An example from the TEV can be seen in the substitution of the word "death," when speaking of Christ's atonement, for the word "blood" (the latter word being the literal rendering of the Greek). Van Bruggen has seen a betrayal of the original Biblical content in this method and protests that,

> When the translator starts reducing the author's form . . . the possibility of letting his own theological prejudice influence the determination of what is essential and what is not essential is far greater than when he sticks as closely as possible to the textual form handed down.[7]

This "sticking as closely as possible to the textual form handed down" has been the method used from the very beginning of Bible translation until recently and in contrast to dynamic-equivalence, it is called formal-equivalence.

For example, if Colossians 1:14 says: "in whom we have redemption through his blood, even the forgiveness of sins" (KJV/KJ21), it is not proper to render this: "in whom we have redemption through his death, even the forgiveness of sins," as Nida and the *Good News Bible* advocate.

According to the teaching of Scripture itself there is grave theological significance to Christ shedding his blood, not just in his death alone, and herein lies the rather substantial problem of dynamic-equivalence: it allows the content and the form of Scripture to capitulate to the language, forms, and culture of the given receptor peoples, even at the loss of Biblical teaching itself.

Again, I am not advocating a total ignoring of the phenomenon of idiom, overdone by Luther and nearly ignored by the *Revised Version* of 1881-83.

Idiom has always been a consideration in traditional,

formal-equivalence translation. Rather, what I am arguing for is that the language, form, and images of Scripture, when translated formally in the traditional sense, do justice to the intent of Scripture, and that is to convert not only personalities, but language and culture, to the matrix of the Judeo-Christian revelation.

We determine this from the first trans-language conveyance of revelational communication from the Old Testament Hebrew, to the Hellenistic Greek of the Septuagint (LXX). F. F. Bruce has established the importance of realizing that,

> the Greek was not suited for Hebrew revelation but was adapted to Hebrew thought forms and transformed by them: To one accustomed to reading good Greek, Septuagint Greek reads very oddly, but to a Greek reader acquainted with Hebrew idiom, Septuagint Greek is immediately intelligible. The words are Greek, but the construction is Hebrew.[8]

Concerning the influence of this Hebraic-Greek of

the LXX on the New Testament, Bruce further mentions that,

> The most important kind of influence exercised by the Septuagint on the New Testament Greek is in the meaning of certain theological and ethical terms. The Greek outlook on religion and morals differed from that of the Jews, and the Greek terms were of course devised and used to reflect the Greek outlook. But the Septuagint translators used these terms to represent Hebrew words which reflected the Jewish outlook, *and thus gave these Greek terms a new connotation*. And it is this new connotation which regularly attaches to these words when they are used in the New Testament [*emphasis mine*].[9]

If this is transformation, or conversion, if you will, of the New Testament Greek, in the direction of revelational content, why should we not see this as the proper approach to translation?

Endnotes Chapter Seven

1 James Deane, "Converting by Translating," *Reformed Journal* vol. 29 (February 1979): pp. 2-3.

2 Noel K. Weeks, *The New Testament Student and Bible Translation* (Philadelphia: The Presbyterian and Reformed Publishing Company, 1978).

3 Jakob Van Bruggen, *The Future of the Bible* (Nashville: Thomas Nelson, Inc., 1978).

4 Eugene A. Nida, *Message and Mission* (New York: Harper and Brothers Publishers, 1960), p. 59.

5 Daane, "Converting by Translating," pp. 1-2.

6 *Ibid.*

7 Van Bruggen, *The Future*, p. 167.

8 F. F. Bruce, *The Books and the Parchments* (London: Pickering and Inglis, Ltd., 1950), p. 70. 52 Ibid., p. 70.

9 *Ibid.*

EIGHT

- *The Renaissance / Reformation Approach to Translation (Theological)* -

Returning to the Renaissance /Reformation period which was, in fact, the birth of modern vernacular Bible translation, we again find a model for this transformation of the receptor language when used to convey revelation, in Luther's German Bible (1534).

Luther not only gave the German people the Bible, (faithful to their idiom, yes, but *not* to the neglect of the original Greek and Hebrew content overall), he greatly influenced German usage, thus giving birth to, and molding the German language around Biblical terms and themes. Goodspeed has noted this:

> Luther's translation was so well done that it went far to form the basis of German as a

literary language; it is generally regarded as the beginning of German literature. It set so high a standard that for centuries no further efforts to translate the Bible into German were made; they seemed superfluous.[1]

Are we hearing Goodspeed right when he says Luther "set the standard" for German literature? Why, this is the very inversion of what Nida advocates when he says Scripture should be reduced to the culture, rather than to mold, or to convert the culture (i.e., language, etc.), to the content and expression of Scripture.

One final example will be offered in our *Authorized Version* of 1611. It has been universally acclaimed as the pinnacle of English expression and the standard by which all great English Literature has been judged.

No one has analyzed this phenomenon with more insight than did C.S., Lewis, in his *The Literary Impact of the Authorised Version*, but many will be amazed to learn that though Lewis acknowledges that it was, indeed, this *Authorized Version* which has had inestimable influence on English language and literature (which is a further substantiation of our thesis that Bible translations should influence culture in its direction, rather than vice versa), he sees this not as a result of seventeenth-century English style, but rather as a result of the "faithful" formal-equivalence translation of the Hebrew and Greek:

> There is . . . no possibility of considering the literary impact of the Authorized Version apart from that of the Bible in general. Except in a few places where the translation is bad, the Authorized Version *owes to the original its matter, its images, and its figures* [*emphasis mine*].[2]

That is to say, because the seventeenth-century Anglican divines who produced the AV held to a high, orthodox view of inspiration, which believed every word, and even syntax was inspired, those merits which we sense intuitively in their Bible are actually the Greek and Hebrew shining through the transparency of the "Biblical" English they employed.

In light of these historical testimonies to the influence which formal-equivalence translation has had when given reign in a culture, Nida's emphasis, and that of nearly all modern Bible publishers' rhetoric, appears hopelessly novel and defective.

Endnotes Chapter Eight

1 Edgar J. Goodspeed, *How Came the Bible?* (Nashville: Abingdon Press, 1940), p. 93.

2 C.S. Lewis, *The Literary Impact of the Authorised Version* (Philadelphia: Fortress Press, 1967), p. 3.

NINE

– Historical Cycles and the Modern Situation –

The English Biblical scholar, F. J. A. Hort once made the observation that Protestant Christianity as we know it today, ". . . is only parenthetical and temporary." Any student of church history would have to concur with his observation.

The renewed Christianity of the sixteenth-century gained a hard-earned peace and freedom which it has experienced since the triumph of the Reformation in the West; and though it may sound paradoxical, it is not suited to such leisure.

Historically, the purest form of Christianity tends to thrive in a persecuted state. It was Tertullian, one of the early church fathers, who said that it was "the blood of the martyrs that was the seed of the church."[1]

If one could draw a principle that best bears this out from church history, it would be that persecution produces a pure form of Christianity which, in turn, becomes adopted by the persecuting powers and thus it then loses its power and purity; then the cycle begins again when persecution is permitted to come and purge the church back to its pure state.

The "blood of the martyrs" purchased the freedom of Christianity from "Imperial" Rome when Constantine adopted Christianity in AD 313.[2]

Just prior to the Protestant Reformation (speaking in broad terms) a decadent form of late medieval Christianity prevailed.

With the reassertion of a more *biblical* Christianity (still speaking in broad terms), Luther and the Reformers suffered great persecution from "Catholic" Rome, until at last Protestant freedom was purchased by "the blood of the martyrs."

It is under this present "parenthetical phase" that we are again entangled with an aberrant form of Christianity, which explains why the publishing of a Bible can be reduced solely to a money-making proposition.

The Bible has in our age passed from the oversight of the Church, into the hands of corporate Bible landlords, each with their own copyrighted editions of Holy Writ.

The *Authorized Version* is the one supreme treasure left to us from the last period of renewal, the very era that purchased our freedom, and it is meant to be a constant reminder of what is the true nature of Christianity. The AV translators still had fresh impressions of the Marian persecution at Smithfield.

Without in any way wanting to needlessly invoke old sectarian animosities, nevertheless, it is important to understand the ethos from which the AV arose.

This intensely emotional feeling is conveyed in the "Letter of Dedication to the King" (still found in many editions of the AV) in which the translators make reference to the freshly won victory over medieval religion. Here they speak in terms of the truth prevailing over the Pope, ". . . which hath given such a blow unto that man of sin, as will not be healed . . ." They also invoked the tendency of the old church to thwart distribution of the Scriptures to the common man:

So that if, on the one side, we shall be traduced by Popish persons at home or abroad, who therefore will malign us, because we are poor instruments to make God's Holy truth to be yet more and more known unto the people whom they desire still to keep in ignorance and darkness . . . we may rest secure, supported within by the truth . . . . [3]

Scholars agree that the AV is virtually the work of William Tyndale (the AV is nine-tenths his version),[4] and as such, it is a blood-stained book in one respect, because Tyndale sealed his work with his death at the stake. His parting prayer was for God to open the eyes of the King of England so that he might grant to the people the freedom to read the Bible in their own language.[5]

That prayer was answered, but how insignificant such freedom seems to most of us today, particularly as a result of the cheapening of the Biblical text in the hands of so many religious merchandisers.

The AV, on the other hand, has for 400 years been our link with the conservative Anglican Reformation heritage and as such represents a William Tyndale type of Christianity; and if given the choice to embrace the type of Christianity historically produced by the AV (if I may be allowed to speak in such terms), or the type that has been produced since the arrival of "the Bible in the language of the people," I feel constrained to embrace the former, archaisms and all.

Not only does the AV supply a Christian with a sense of identity by giving him a direct link with his Protestant roots, and the *via media* of the English Reformation, but it also undergirds this sense of identity by supplying him with a unifying force for the present.

For example, there is a popular misconception that the name *Authorized Version* was given to the 1611 edition because of some official decree given by King James, but this just was not so.

King James merely gave permission for the translation to take place only after he was asked by John Reynolds, one of the translators. "Strictly speaking, the authorized version was never authorized, nor were parish churches ordered to procure it."[6] It seems to have acquired the title on its own merit!

This common consensus is so well established it hardly requires to be labored. F.F. Bruce acknowledged that,

> it is well recognized that, throughout the English speaking world, there are hundreds of thousands of readers by whom this version [the AV] is accepted as 'The Word of God' in a sense in which no other version would be accepted.[7]

It has also been described as having "acquired a sanctity properly ascribable only to the unmediated voice of God."[8] The most telling summation, however, both of the unifying effect of the AV, as well as its ability to command authority, was given by Burgon:

> Whatever may be urged in favour of Biblical revision, it is at least undeniable that the undertaking involves a tremendous risk. Our AV is the one religious link which at present binds together ninety millions of English-speaking men scattered over the earth's surface. Is it

reasonable that so unutterably precious, so sacred a bond should be endangered, for the sake of representing certain words more accurately — here and there translating a tense with greater precision — getting rid of a few archaisms? It may be confidently assumed that no revision of our AV, however judiciously executed, will ever occupy the place in publick [sic] esteem which is actually enjoyed by the work of the translators of 1611 — the noblest literary work in the Anglo-Saxon language. We shall in fact never have *another* "Authorized Version."[9]

Another illustration of the AV's ability to command authority to the popular mind is seen in the Gideon Bible found in most hospitals and motels. In spite of all the Madison Avenue talk about "more reliable manuscripts" the Gideons still publish the AV text as their Bible. The Gideons have seen them all come and go over the years, from the first *Revised Version* in 1883, to the present "superstar," *The New International Version*, and to date, it is still the AV that holds sway over the popular mind.[10]

With so much discussion about the need for unity in the church one would think that more people would recognize the value of the AV to this end, but instead one hears only of using "the Bible of your choice," which tends to lead to fragmentation in any group study, rather than to unity.

The results of having an abundance of modern versions to choose from are anything but constructive. According to an article in the *New York Times*, within the past twenty years "several hundred versions of the Bible, catering to every niche of reader" has resulted in a glut in the market, "too many Bibles for too few faithful."[11]

The obvious problem of conflicting translations is illustrated by the many books that follow in the wake of the many translations, which attempt to clarify why there are so many translations! A few titles are, *Why So Many Bibles?*, 1968; *What Bible Can You Trust?*, 1974; *Which Bible?*, 1975; *So Many Versions?*, 1975; and others.

John 1:18 provides a good example of the kind of confusion that results from conflicting translations. The AV (and the KJ21) reads:

"No man hath seen God at any time; *The Only Begotten Son*, Which is in the bosom of the Father, He hath declared Him."

The italicized portion of the verse is rendered in the following different ways by some modern versions:

NIV and TEV
"The only Son"
["begotten" omitted]

NASB
"The Only Begotten God" [Polytheism?]

NEB
"God's Only Son"
["begotten" omitted and "God" added]

Which is correct?[12]

As for the footnotes in the modern versions, they seem to be questioning the authenticity of every other verse with comments such as "not found in some ancient manuscripts" or "some manuscripts add," without offering any explanation as to the value of these optional readings, or the various manuscripts they come from.

This tends to leave the average reader (unconsciously perhaps) with a doubtful attitude regarding what he can consider authoritative and in some sense final. Burgon noted this when such footnotes were first employed in the RV (1881):

The marginal readings, which our revisers have been so ill-advised as to put prominently forward, and to introduce to the reader's notice with the vague statement that they are sanctioned by 'some' (or by 'Many') 'ancient authorities', — are specimens *arbitrarily selected* out of an immense mass . . . . No hint is given as to *which be* the 'ancient authorities' so referred to: — nor what proportion they bear to the ancient authorities producible on the opposite side: — nor whether they are even the *most* 'ancient authorities' obtainable: — nor what amount of attention their testimony may reasonably claim . . . . How comes it to pass that you have . . . instead, volunteered in every page information, worthless in itself, which can only serve to unsettle the faith of unlettered millions, and to suggest unreasonable as well as miserable doubts to the minds of all?[13]

We have become so desensitized by these notes in our modern editions that one can hardly appreciate the impact they must have had on the first generation to encounter them in the *Revised Version* (1883).

An example that might be able to shake us afresh will serve to illustrate just how misleading such footnotes can be.

At Mark 16:9-20, in the *New International Version*, there is a footnote stating, "The most reliable early manuscripts omit Mark 16:9-20." What they fail to make clear is that out of the approximately 5,487[14] Greek manuscripts available to scholars, of those that contain Mark, only three manuscripts omit this passage.

Two of them, *Vaticanus* and *Sinaiticus*, were put to the most detailed study of perhaps any others to date, by

Herman Hoskier, in his *Codex B and Its Allies: A Study and an Indictment* (1914).

No man in his day, nor perhaps since, knew these two documents as intimately as did Hoskier. The conclusion of his study offered the following consensus:

> To revive the Egyptian textual standard [represented by Codices Vaticanus and Sinaiticus] of A.D. 200-400 is not scientific, and it is certainly not final. The truth is scattered over all our documents and is not inherent entirely in any one document, nor in any two. Hort persuaded himself that where א B were together... they must be right. This kind of fetishism must be done away with.[15]

Endnotes Chapter Nine

1 Earle E. Cairns, *Christianity Through the Centuries*, 6th ed. (Grand Rapids: Zondervan Publishing House, 1973), p. 72.

2 B.K. Kuiper, *The Church In History* (Grand Rapids: The National Union of Christian Schools, Eerdmans, 1975), p. 24.

3 Oxford or Cambridge Editions of the Authorized Version. Citing this provocative document should not be interpreted as a piece of Protestant triumphalism, particularly in light of the historical record of *misapplication* of Scripture once placed in the hands of Protestant communities, i.e., the burning of Michael Servetus at the hands of the Genevan Calvinists, the slaughter of the peasants under Luther's watchful eye, and the regicide at the hands of the English Puritans. Rather, it is intended to be honest about the historical ethos from which the 1611 edition came forth.

4 Neil R. Lightfoot, *How We Got the Bible* (Grand Rapids: Baker Book House, 1974), p. 101.

5 *Ibid.*, p. 99.
What Tyndale meant by in their "own language" was *English*, rather than *Latin*, *not* conversational colloquialism!

6 S.L. Greenslade, ed., *The Cambridge History of the Bible*, 3 vols. (London: Cambridge University Press), "*The West From the Reformation to the Present,*" p. 168.

7 Bruce, *The English Bible*, p. 112.

8 Greenslade, *The Cambridge History*, p. 168.

9 John W. Burgon, *The Revision Revised*, 2nd ed. (London: John Murray, 1885), p. 113.

10 They do, however, supply modern language versions on special request.

Endnotes Chapter Nine Continued

11 Doreen Carvajal, "The Bible, a Perennial, Runs into Sales Resistance," *New York Times* (October 28, 1996).

12 For a detailed and technical treatment of this variant, see Theodore P. Letis, "The Gnostic Influences on the Text of the Fourth Gospel: John 1:18 in the Egyptian Manuscripts and the Canonical Approach," in *The Ecclesiastical Text: Textual Criticism, Biblical Authority and the Popular Mind* (Institute for Reformation Biblical Studies, 1997).

13 Burgon, *The Revision Revised*, pp. 131, 130.

14 Graham Stanton, *Gospel Truth: New Light on Jesus and the Gospels* (HarperCollins, 1995), p. 37.

15 Hoskier, *Codex B*, vol. 1, p. 487.

- Summary -

In conclusion, the *Authorized Version* should be retained by the churches, as well as in Bible study and in the classroom, because of the superior consensus represented by its Greek text, its translation technique, and its English usage; and because it not only provides the Christian with a link to his Protestant heritage, but it also supplies him with a sense of unifying identity for the present.

I do not believe, however, that anyone has the right, nor the authority, to pontificate to the Christian world *one* Bible alone as Holy Scripture, while anathematizing the rest to the incinerator (the Holy Spirit Himself must ultimately bear witness to the Divine final authority).

We have all heard testimonies of people who have come to the Christian faith by reading a Jehovah's

Witness Bible. Martin Luther received salvation light from a Roman Catholic Latin Vulgate. We should never think that the Holy Spirit is limited to Elizabethan English.

Nevertheless, to whom much is given, much will be required. Those of us who have become aware that the modern Bibles represent more the abstract concerns emanating from the competing textual theories of various specialists, as well as representing the more pragmatic concerns of the Bible marketing industry which has capitalized on the loss of consensus produced by the specialists, it would seem we have a responsibility. That is, to direct young and seeking pilgrims, as well as seasoned saints, back to the "old landmarks."

John Wesley stated it this way:

I have thought, I am a creature of a day, passing through life as an arrow through the air. I am a spirit come from God, and returning to God: just hovering over the great gulf; till, a few moments hence, I am no more seen; I drop into an unchangeable eternity! I want to know one thing — the way to heaven; how to land safe on that happy shore. God Himself has condescended to teach the way; for this very end He came from heaven. He hath written it down in a Book. O, give me that Book! At any price, give me *the* Book of God!" [*emphasis mine*]

veritas temporis filia

About the Author

Theodore P. Letis (1951-2005) (PhD, Edinburgh University; MTS, Emory University) was director of the Institute for Renaissance and Reformation Biblical Studies, president of the University of Edinburgh Theological Society and a member of the Society of Biblical Literature, the American Academy of Religion, and the American Society of Church History. He authored *The Ecclesiastical Text: Text Criticism, Biblical Authority and the Popular Mind* and was editor and contributor to *The Majority Text: Essays and Reviews in the Continuing Debate*.

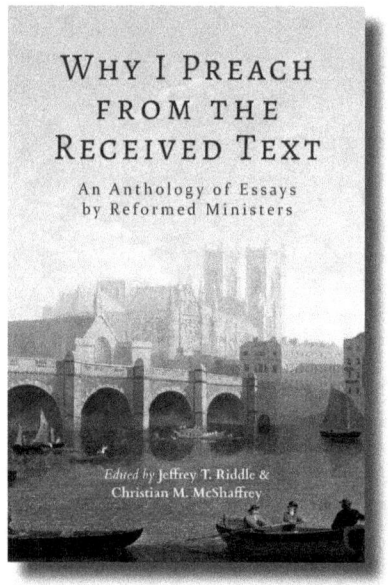

www.ingramcontent.com/pod-product-compliance
Lightning Source LLC
Chambersburg PA
CBHW071213120626
46546CB00006B/2548